Invitation to
ARCHAEOLOGY

INVITATION SERIES

Other titles in preparation

Invitation to
ARCHAEOLOGY

Philip Rahtz

BASIL BLACKWELL

First published 1985
Basil Blackwell Ltd
108 Cowley Road, Oxford OX4 1JF, UK

Basil Blackwell Inc.
432 Park Avenue South, Suite 1505,
New York, NY 10016, USA

British Library Cataloguing in Publication Data
Rahtz, Philip
Invitation to archaeology—(Invitation series)
1. Archaeology
I. Title
930.1   CC165 . *R34*

49,051

ISBN 0–631–14106–5
ISBN 0–631–14107–3 Pbk

Typeset by Katerprint Co. Ltd, Oxford
Printed in Great Britain by
T.J. Press Ltd, Padstow

Contents

Preface

This book is written towards the end of a professional career in archaeology. This did not begin until I was over 30, so it has been short compared with that of the average academic. I began as an amateur, and shall to some extent revert to that status after retirement. At this stage in my life I can afford to be honest, uninhibited, and indiscreet in expounding my beliefs. I can let my hair down (what little remains) without needing to mind the consequent ridicule. I can be nostalgic, sentimental, garrulous, anecdotal, prejudiced, and inaccurate (as any semi-autobiographical book is bound to be).

Fortunately, this is what Basil Blackwell seemed to want. The *Invitation* series was not intended to be a collection of even more textbooks, and this book is certainly not in that category. Its intention is to show that archaeology is important to people and to society, it is immensely stimulating and educational, and will enrich the life of anybody who becomes involved in it.

My audience is anyone who feels mildly interested in or curious about archaeology, and wants to know more: the school-leaver wondering whether to study the subject at university level; the adult thinking of joining an evening class or an excavation; those with enforced (or voluntary) leisure, looking for some rewarding way of using their time; those already subscribing to popular archaeological magazines; or even those on treasure-hunting, ley-lines, or metal-detecting expeditions – see Chapter 7; anyone wanting to know more about archaeology, but unwilling to read a serious textbook; and my academic colleagues in search of light relief.

I have had very few original ideas in my life (though I have invented some new jokes), so I am indebted to a very large number of people I have met in the course of my digging and academic career, whose ideas, remarks, and attitudes I have absorbed and distorted. I will name only those who are currently influential in preserving me from worse excesses: my colleagues in the Department of Archaeology at York, Tania Dickinson, Harold Mytum and Steve Roskams; my secretary, Priscilla Roxburgh; Ann Ellison, Sue Hirst, Peter Leach, and Martin Carver; my York students, past and present; my colleague Edward James, who has read the whole book in draft, and made valuable comments; Ian Burrow, who has allowed his humour to be immortalized; my wife Lorna Watts; Carole Barrowclough, who has coped with my typing; and finally Kim Pickin at Basil Blackwell, who invited me to write this book.

This is not the first book on archaeology to have this title. James Deetz wrote his classic in 1967, which has been used by students all over the world. My only excuse for plagiarizing his title is that mine is one of Basil Blackwell's *Invitation* series; I hope he will find it a worthy namesake.

May I finally stress that 'he', 'man', 'mankind' and other male-oriented words in this book apply equally to women.

1

What is Archaeology?

Archaeology is the study of material culture in its relationship to human behaviour – the physical manifestations of man's activities, his rubbish and his treasure, his buildings and his graves. It is also concerned with the environment in which mankind has developed and in which man still lives. This may include factors over which he has little or no control, such as sunspots, climate, and tides; it may also include the ways in which man among other animals (but to a vastly greater extent than, for example, beavers) has transformed the landscape, the animal world, and recently the atmosphere; and the chemistry of sea, lake and river.

Archaeologists thus study not only pots and jewellery, temples and tombs, ditches and mounds, but also lake sediments, beetles, animal bones, excrement, and parasites. They are normally interested in past societies, but it is important to note that these definitions do not exclude the study of today's material culture. Some archaeologists study the contents of dustbins, notably in Tucson, Arizona (the 'garbage project', Rathje, 1978). It's true that archaeology is mostly about the past, as its name implies; but when this is the case, the archaeologist is really being a historian, using this word to mean anyone who is interested in the past, rather than someone who studies documents. To make any sense of past material remains, however, archaeology has to have *theory*, concerning what can or cannot be deduced from material residues (i.e. 'rubbish'). Archaeologists are as much concerned nowadays with developing theory as are scientists. This can be done by studying modern material culture as well as that surviving from past societies (Chapter 6).

We can live in an African village or in a modern city and formulate and test theory: do the dustbins of Tucson really reflect the ethnic and class divisions of the city? Can we reconstruct the vice-chancellor's lifestyle from his dustbin and compare it with that of the self-catering undergraduate? The short answer is yes, there is a demonstrable relationship: the VC drinks more expensive wine and eats more meat than the undergraduate; this is indicated by the bottles and bones in his dustbin.

With such improved theoretical understanding, and with the arsenal of techniques that archaeology can now deploy, we can attempt to reconstruct past human behaviour. This has in the past tended to be mainly descriptive. We have been successful in showing how people buried their dead, what their churches and temples were like, how they farmed the land, and what food they ate. This is all very well, and of intrinsic interest, but nowadays archaeology is more ambitious: it seeks to deduce not only *what* happened, but *why* it happened. Why, at some times and in some places, do people cremate their dead, rather than bury them? Why has cremation gained ground *(sic)* so rapidly in the twentieth century? Why did towns develop? Did past populations increase or decrease because of climatic changes, or improved technology, or a changing economy, or combinations of several causes?

WHY ARCHAEOLOGY?

Why should anyone want to know about the past? Most people are interested only in the present, so why should a small minority be so concerned about origins and change? Answers to these weighty questions are difficult, but the reader will, it is hoped, have a better understanding after reading this book. The question, 'Why do people do archaeology?' is explored in Chapter 2. At this point in the book, we may anticipate the discussion by concluding that there are two principal reasons. It is done for enjoyment, and/or because it is actually important.

I should straightaway declare my firm belief that not only is archaeology fun and highly educational and intellectually satisfying to the individual, it is also crucial to the survival of man on this planet, and should be accorded high priority and resources by modern society. Understanding of man's past is an important aid to understanding people today. It is the one subject (though others make similar claims) which is central to all knowledge, with hot lines to all other disciplines. As such it affords the Great Perspective from which we need to take a cool, balanced look at our own society.

How can archaeology claim such a centrality among the humanities? Principally (and here also lies its immense educational value) it is precisely because of its links with other disciplines. Archaeology is not a science like biology or chemistry, though it uses scientific methods and adopts scientific attitudes. It has been described as a cultural science, and has in recent years been moving closer to the social sciences than to the natural ones, for reasons that I hope will become apparent. Modern archaeology finds increasingly common ground with anthropology, philosophy, sociology, and politics. It is really aiming at the same thing – the understanding of humans – by utilizing the special method of the interpretation of material residues. The obvious limitations of such an approach are that it is difficult to find out from material remains such as ruins and cesspit residues what men think or thought, a factor regarded as central to the other social sciences. Archaeology's great advantage is however that, unlike these disciplines, it can bring an enriched and broader time dimension to the study of man. The observation of the minds of living man (as in the social sciences) can to some extent be extended by written sources, which are the special province of historians. These are, however, available for only the most recent past of man – a few thousand years at most, and in some parts of the world no more than a few generations. The archaeologist is concerned with a time-scale

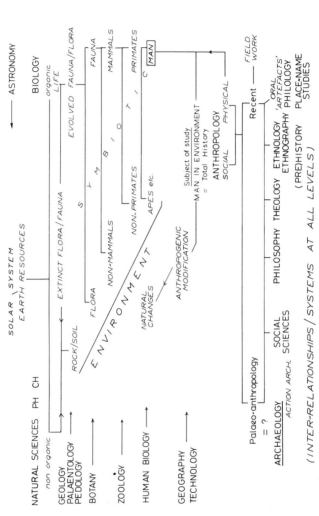

Figure 1 Archaeology and other subjects 1.

thousands of times longer – up to five million years in Africa and the Far East, and tens of thousands in even the most recently settled areas, such as Australia or America; only in remote and relatively inaccessible places, such as New Zealand, is the time-span to be measured only in the hundreds of years normally available to the students of written sources. Archaeology's interests cover the entire world, from Samoa to Spain, from Australia to North America; and in material from fossil hominid bones and stone tools to today's dust-bins.

ARCHAEOLOGY AND OTHER SUBJECTS

Subjects concerned with the origins of the world and life provide our understanding both of the environment and of the complex biological evolution which peopled it with man, plants and other life-forms (Figures 1 and 2). Although man evolves as part of this environment, and is studied within it, increasingly he alters it (anthropogenic modification). This results from the profound effects of his activities on the environment (by pollution, desiccation, etc.), and also by his direct exploitation of natural resources. Large areas of the present world landscape owe their appearance to the patterns imposed by farming, industry, towns and communications.

The most important subject with which archaeology is linked (and which it is part of) is anthropology. *Physical* anthropology deals with both the biology of living man (for example, the study of racial types, etc.), and also with the remains of past man made available by archaeology. *Social* anthropology, on the other hand, is concerned primarily not with *palaeo*-anthropology (=archaeology), but with recent man as studied through the social sciences, theology, language, history and other allied disciplines. Because of the material available for their study, it is only rarely that social (or 'cultural') anthropologists are interested in origins, development and change (i.e. the past). All these disciplines contribute to the understanding of man in the environment; only interdisciplinary collaboration can provide maximum

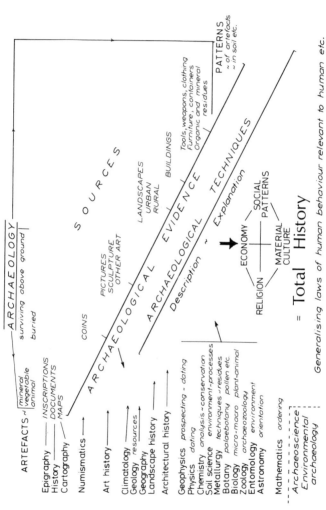

Figure 2 Archaeology and other subjects.

enlightenment. This sounds obvious, but is difficult to bring about in practice, whether in universities or out in the field, because of the blinkered attitude of specialists to disciplines other than their own; (this doubtless applies to archaeologists too, but I am too blinkered to see it).

We could imagine in an ideal future world (and it has occasionally already happened) an expedition to the highlands of New Guinea, consisting of a social and a physical anthropologist, other social scientists, a linguist, an archaeologist, and other scientists concerned with the environment and natural resources. But who would be the director? (The special role here of the ethnographer/ethno-archaeologist will be discussed more fully in Chapter 6.)

Archaeological evidence, in both its buried and above-ground elements, has many categories of sources ranging from small artefacts (such as a pin) to major structures (such as the Taj Mahal or Stonehenge), together with the landscapes in which they are found or survive. Numerous disciplines lend their assistance both to the discovery of this diverse material and to its full understanding. The material, and the patterns which can be discerned across space and time, become the archaeological evidence, which may then be realized by describing and explaining it. The social, economic, and religious framework are the *systems* of society whose interaction must be understood in the context of Total History.

Archaeology may thus be seen as a separate discipline, with its own approaches and methods, heavily dependent on the help of many specialists, but having the special aim of understanding a very long time-span in diverse habitats. Since his interest extends well before the period for which other sources are available, the archaeologist is interested not only in important events, such as those recorded in written documents, but in the whole fabric of society, from the activities of hunter – gatherers to those of town dwellers, from peasants to chieftains, from lakeside villagers to those in desert areas. Archaeology is mostly impersonal, concerned more with societies and trends than individual people.

THE LIMITATIONS OF ARCHAEOLOGY AND
HOW TO OVERCOME THEM

To those who are not interested in archaeology, it appears to have precisely these limitations: it is rarely concerned with named people. Non-archaeologists *like* named people, and their interest in the past rarely extends beyond such real or imaginary people as Julius Caesar or King Arthur. Archaeology also fails to satisfy those people who are interested in the working of men's minds. These limitations of archaeology are at the root of many of the problems discussed in later chapters.

It must be said, in the final part of this chapter, that archaeologists themselves have become increasingly dissatisfied with these limitations to their understanding of the past, and have sought ways, by improved theory or technique, to overcome them. These attempts have dominated the recent history of archaeology, and may be summarized here briefly. In the short history of the subject (a century or two at most) the ambitions of the archaeologist began with the collection, description and classification of artefacts and buildings; they graduated to the delineation of past lifestyles and technological and economic systems; and finally to today's bold aims of understanding not only the environment of earlier man (made possible by dramatic developments in the natural sciences), and the entire interaction of systems in society, but also the structures within the human mind. Some archaeologists (notably Ian Hodder at Cambridge) believe that human minds have a far greater importance in the development of society than what these archaeologists see as the rather mundane factors of climate, environment, and economic or political necessity. The effect of the mind on material remains is of course difficult to gauge from merely examining, for example, patterns on pottery. It can only be shown by ethno-archaeology. An archaeologist may go and live in an African village. He sees pottery being made and decorated. He also (if he is a competent linguist) finds out what people are thinking, what social tensions exist, what group allegiances or feuds are going on. Linking these together, he observes that patterns on pottery have little to do with regional style, religious belief, or custom, but whether Mrs Mgongo is attempting to assert her independence over her stepmother.

Contemporary trends towards such a 'cognitive' approach are ambitious and interesting, and at the least alert the more traditional archaeologist to a wider range of explanation than has hitherto been assumed, in attempts to understand human behaviour from material remains.

ALTERNATIVE INTERPRETATIONS

Archaeologists are not scientists in the text book sense. One reason for this disclaimer is that much of the work they do, and the conclusions they come to, cannot be repeated or tested by someone else. The essence of a scientific experiment is that it can be done again and the same results achieved. This is obviously impossible in archaeology, especially in excavation, as the evidence is destroyed in the process of recovering it. I spent two years excavating the Saxon and medieval palaces at Cheddar in Somerset; I recovered data plans of: post-holes of many great wooden buildings, details of numerous ditches, coins, pottery, metal objects, and bones. From all these I wrote a report (Rahtz, 1979) in which I tried to make sense of all this, working out what had happened at Cheddar, and why, between the ninth and fourteenth centuries AD. In particular, I split everything there into seven separate periods, which I thought represented significant episodes of building construction and activity – times when resources were put into development, in this case principally by the authority of kings or bishops. My seven phases are generally accepted as 'true' (or if they aren't nobody has told me). They are however essentially *my* story, *my* ordering and interpretation of a very diverse and difficult body of evidence, recovered in a hurry and not very skilfully, as the site was to be destroyed by the building of a school.

But what would another archaeologist have found?

Unfortunately we shall never know – I can't put it all back so that someone else can repeat the experiment. The best we can do is to record as much as we can as objectively as possible. Anyone who has been on a dig knows how subjective most of the 'evidence' is, based on where to dig, how to dig it, and what it 'means' (see Chapter 7: How likely is likely?). We can only do our best by at least publishing full data, however subjective, which others can rework. Some well-recorded nineteenth-century excavations have been successfully re-interpreted in the light of modern ideas. After I am dead, I hope that Cheddar can be re-thought from *the data* I have published.

Even if we cannot claim to be scientists, we can try to be as rigorous as possible, by enlisting various specialist skills. It is no good nowadays just recording that 'in this pit were ten Roman sherds and a lot of greenish dirt'. Scientists can describe the dirt accurately and suggest its derivation. Is it human or animal cess? Did it all get put in at once, or drift in very slowly? What is the exact composition of each sherd of pottery? What grits were used, how hot was the kiln? What *is* the evidence for it being Roman?

At the very least, an archaeologist tries to argue his case objectively, and especially logically. What is the evidence, as far as he can discern it? What hypothesis may be put up to explain its 'meaning'? How is this hypothesis to be tested? What alternative hypotheses can be put up, to be tested and possibly rejected in turn? Which seems on balance most likely? Having decided, this one doesn't become 'true'; archaeologists' evasiveness here causes much irritation to scientists and non-scientists alike.

Good archaeologists are logical in what they write in a report (in contrast to wild stories invented at tea-time on the dig), and also essentially rational. This engenders much enmity, because few people like rationality. In Chapter 7 we shall meet some of these enemies, non-rationalists who are more interested in finding proof for their favourite theory about King Arthur, Atlantis, or spacemen building stone circles. Rationalism is the enemy of romance, but to many people the past is, by definition, romantic. This is why archaeologists may find it difficult to sell 500 copies of a monograph representing several years of sustained hard work, while Von Däniken can sell over forty million copies of *Chariots of the Gods?* and its sequels.

We shall also explore the major fallacy about finds. Most people are convinced that archaeologists dig for finds, preferably of gold or silver. Hence the metal detectors' claims that they can 'do archaeology' better than archaeologists. This is, alas, an attitude encouraged by museums (with notable exceptions) and by those who place cash value on archaeological artefacts.

While it is true that many rich and valuable finds, such as those from the tomb of Tutankhamun or Sutton Hoo (Chapter 8), *are* also extremely important archaeologically, they are to an archaeologist only a means to an end, to understanding man's past and not to sell or put on shelves in a collection. To non-archaeologists they are also objects of beauty and rarity, which do have commercial value.

ARCHAEOLOGY AND PEOPLE

Another problem is getting people interested in subjects like past economics, social systems, environments, etc. As we have seen, people are interested in people, hence the appeal of 'Dallas' or 'Coronation Street'. It is curious that the skilful representation of the associated social systems in Texas and Lancashire are ignored. This obsession with our own species as 'people' is known rudely as anthropocentrism. History is vastly more popular than archaeology because named people figure in it quite a lot; not only people but 'interesting' people like kings, generals, prime ministers, dictators and criminals.

Most people in the past who made buildings and pottery, threw away rubbish, and got buried in graves, were none of these things. They were peasants, the submerged nine-tenths whose activities didn't hit the headlines of the Anglo-Saxon Chronicle, and whose very names are mostly unknown.

All people and their activities, their lives and their deaths, are the concern of the archaeologist, in his efforts to understand the five-million year history of mankind. Sadly, to most people this is dull stuff though I hope the reader will not be among them when he has read this book.

If archaeology is so dreary, unromantic, impersonal, and rational, why do archaeologists like it? They are after all ordinary people. Who are they? How did they come to be interested? Who pays them to do it? (Those who sign the cheques must think it worthwhile.) In our next chapter we explore these questions, Who? And why?

2

Motivation, Finance, and Politics

There are many different kinds of archaeologists. They range from the most abstruse kinds of theorist, concerned only with ideas on the abstract relationship between material residues and human behaviour (close to philosophers in their interests in the structure of knowledge), to the unemployed labourer on an excavation. Mortimer Wheeler asked one of the latter what he found most interesting in the work; the reply was, not surprisingly, 'the five o'clock whustle'!

Academics like myself think, do and teach archaeology, and we provide the framework of learning and doing for graduate and undergraduate students (Chapter 5). In Britain the total number of university lecturers in archaeology is relatively small, no more than a few hundred. Other archaeologists are employed in fully professional units, such as in York or London; each of these is currently working on a budget of about half a million pounds, and with a staff of a hundred or more. They may work under the aegis of a university department such as that at Durham, or of a local government authority such as the unit at Carlisle. In all cases much of the finance comes from central government, but 'privatization' is increasing. In Western Europe there are major state or regional research institutes, such as the Dutch State Archaeological Service, or the province-based institutes in North West Germany. These are more academically-linked than those in Britain, and some are directly organized in

13

relation to university research, such as the Institute for Pre- and Proto-history at the University of Amsterdam. Smaller numbers of professionals work in the Ordnance Survey, mapping antiquities; or in the Royal Commission on Historical Monuments, recording landscapes, structures and buildings. The staff of museums are employed principally in collecting, conserving and displaying the objects and results of archaeology; but some, such as the British Museum, sponsor or organize field-work in Britain or overseas; and many museums do employ full-time archaeologists to look after the archaeology of their local area.

There are professional freelance archaeologists, making a living from digging (as I did for ten years), lecturing on Hellenic cruises, writing books, appearing on TV or radio, and especially working on the publication of archaeological reports (there is a big backlog here of non-published excavations). There are also many amateurs. Their role and status (invaluable help or menace) varies from country to country. In Britain there is a very strong amateur tradition going back over a century to the founding of regional archaeological societies. They help on excavations, in museums, and in field survey. For many their stimulus comes from attending extramural classes. Most are content to do routine work such as pot-washing, cataloguing, or digging. Some have higher aspirations, and there are a number whose work rates alongside that of academics or field professionals. Don Spratt, for instance, in my own area, retired in his fifties from a post as research leader in ICI, enrolled at Sheffield University as a mature student, and went on to do important field work in North Yorkshire, and to publish his results to the highest professional standards. The amateur involvement in Wharram Percy, in East Yorkshire, has been fundamental to its success, and will be more fully discussed in Chapter 8.

The range of people engaged in archaeology in other countries is similar to that in Britain, but certain differences will become apparent later in this chapter when we look at political and other motivations. It should be noted that archaeologists don't work only in their own countries. There are British Schools or Institutes in several places in Europe such as Rome, Athens, Ankara, and Jerusalem; and other countries, especially Germany, Italy, France, and the USA, have mounted major expeditions abroad, notably in the fields of Greco-Roman and Holy Land archaeology. There is also 'colonial' archaeology, such as that of the French in Algeria and Tunisia, the English and French in Egypt when it was under Anglo-French mandate, and the English in India.

WHY DO PEOPLE DO ARCHAEOLOGY?

Motivations are private and public, academic and commercial. I will list these, and then, in a brief world tour, see what is characteristic of different areas, and (in Chapter 3) how many apply in Britain. I have ranged them in an order of 'respectability' (ranging from the purely academic to the frankly sinister), but I do not expect my readers to agree with this ranking, which clearly reflects my own cultural prejudices.

(1) Intellectual curiosity and the pursuit of knowledge for its own sake. This is a recognized and valid activity of human beings, and one which should be supported by public or private funds. It is, however, increasingly under attack by governments with an eye to economic gain and 'social relevance'.

(2) The expansion of the data-base of anthropology or ethnology. This is closely allied to (1), but may be easier to argue than straight archaeology, being related to existing rather than dead peoples.

(3) The provision of data about the past to help us to predict and change the future. Can politicians learn from history or archaeology and avoid making the same mistakes? To paraphrase a well-known quotation: 'the only thing we learn from archaeology is that people never learn anything from archaeology.'

(4) Public education: giving everybody a wider perspective of man's past, helping them to live in the world today, and at the least enriching their lives in their visits to ancient monuments and museums. This is the great 'cultural heritage'

15

bandwagon, on to which many archaeologists are now climbing.

(5) The promotion of tourism, with attendant financial gain. There is a grey area between this and (4) above. Tourist-related archaeology at its best can be highly educational, and it can present a totally authentic picture of the past. York's new Jorvik Viking Centre recreates a Viking townscape with people – and everything visible to the public in their slowly-moving 'time cars', the sounds they hear, or the foul smells around them, is evidenced by archaeology, history or language. Indeed it could be said that tourist-orientated displays are *the* principal means of bringing archaeology to the widest public, whether in museums, reconstructed buildings, cathedral treasuries, or, best of all, the great folk-parks of Scandinavia, Ulster, Wales, and the USA. Sturbridge Old Village, near Boston, Massachusetts, has a 20 ha site where we see an early nineteenth-century village in action, with church, mill, carpenter's shop, pottery kiln, farm, eating-house, and church. Everyone is in costume, doing, making or serving. A million visitors a year pay seven dollars entry fee, and spend as much again in the shop, which sells all the things made in the village; you can furnish your home entirely in early Puritan style. Thirty-four staff are employed, including an archaeologist. The appeal is wide, satisfying the ordinary American in search of roots and nostalgia, and also the visiting foreign archaeologist interested in New England culture.

The result then of tourism–orientation is often excellent in its results, if not always in its motivation; at worst it can be highly misleading and a total rip-off. Archaeology has to be cost-effective and money-spinning to survive, and this in England is the philosophy behind the new Historical Buildings and Monuments Commission. Our monuments should be made attractive, while hopefully avoiding scandals such as Stonehenge, where public car-parks, lavatories and wire disfigure the open landscape of Salisbury Plain, and where one cannot even touch the stones. The York Archaeological Trust uses the profits of its commercial arm (significantly named Cultural Resource Management) to finance its research in the archaeology of the city.

(6) The establishment of a common basis in the past for what may appear now to be highly disparate cultures or linguistic groups, such as those of the USSR. Archaeology, by means of public education in museums, plays a valuable role in demonstrating to Russians that if one goes back far enough in time, Russia has a unified past.

(7) The definition of ethnic identity and cultural roots, or even (at worst) of ethnic superiority. This may be used either to create a national identity or to stimulate 'lost' national pride; or more aggressively to justify subjugation or colonization of 'inferior' peoples – many examples will be cited later in this chapter.

(8) The justification of male or female dominance. The ball has in the past been mainly in the male court – man is the food-hunter, the strong protector, the builder, the king, the pope, and so on – but increasingly the results of ethnographic or archaeological research may be cited to support feminist claims that females are more crucial to the survival of the species. It is they who provide the *regular* food supply by gathering and later by farming (hunters often fail), who succour the children, who invent. Patriarchal, male-dominated societies may be a relatively recent phenomenon, and examples may be found in ethnography of societies where women take on all the 'male' roles of politicians, landowners, warriors, or priests. *Scientific American* (January 1972) carried a drawing to illustrate the idea that women should be as free as men to pursue educational and occupational goals. Archaeology is chosen to illustrate this. A woman in jacket and trousers is shown reclining on an easy chair with her feet on a stool. She is reading a heavily-thumbed copy of *Archaeologia* and day-dreaming. In the background her dream is illustrated. Women on dream-clouds, in similar dress, are working on an ancient temple site. One has a geologist's hammer (?) another a long rod (?) probing or measuring, another is poring over strange inscriptions on clay tablets, and a fourth is pounding away on a typewriter.

(9) The establishment of data-sets on which to test out hypotheses. It has been said that American archaeologists

investigating Indian archaeology in the USA do so not out of interest in Indian culture (least of all for the benefit of Indians), but to provide fodder for computer analysis. Unlike Europeans, they cannot identify with the people whose settlements and graves they are digging up, Arkansas is, however, nearer to home than Greece, where they'd *really* like to work if they had the money!

(10) The support of myth by invoking the 'scientific' support of archaeology. This is something I have had direct experience of, having dug at Glastonbury for five seasons. The material under this heading is so rich as to be worth the full treatment it is going to get in Chapter 7.

(11) The validation of religious truth. Wheeler called Palestine 'the land of original archaeological sin', the implication being that much of what purported to be scientific archaeology, 'proving the truth' of the Old or New Testament, was not only bad archaeology, but grossly biased in its interpretation towards what the expedition or its sponsors wished to prove. Other examples are the expeditions to Mount Ararat to find Noah's Ark, or the excavations at Tara in Ireland by the British Israelites in 1912 to dig up the Ark of the Covenant. In the latter case, enormous damage was done to one of Tara's most important earthworks, which left very little for a later Irish excavator.

(12) The building-up of the ego or the public image of the individual or institution. The former has been my own primary motivation, and I suspect not as absent from even the academic archaeological scene as we would like to think. This is often, for the individual, related to promoting career prospects, or for the institution to securing financial sponsorship. Any museum that buys treasures looted from tombs provides the most inexcusable instances in this category.

Slightly more respectable is the removal of objects to a 'safe' place from some 'backward' country, which cannot look after its cultural heritage. In the case of the Benin Bronzes, this was no more than legalized looting, but Elgin did believe he was saving the Parthenon marble frieze, and he was right, insofar as the fragments in the British Museum are the only ones which are now in good condition, Athenian pollution having severely eroded the rest. He did also obtain them in an entirely legal way. But now that the Greeks have proper conditions to look after them, Melina Mercouri is in my view fully justified in demanding them back, and here I cross swords with my eminent colleague Sir David Wilson, the Director of the British Museum.

(13) The search for treasure or other loot, including art-objects, for the royal or aristocratic purse, or for the enrichment of private or museum collections. This is a very ancient motivation, going back in England to our medieval monarchs who ordered barrows to be dug for gold. It is highly prevalent today all over the world, sometimes done in ignorance (as with many metal-detector enthusiasts), but often with full cognizance of the damage done to sites and robbing us of our cultural heritage.

A WORLD TOUR

In this brief survey of case-studies of the good and bad motivations that inspire archaeology in various countries, we are examining principally *public* archaeology. By that I mean work which has been financed from public funds, and which has therefore been thought valid and useful to society by those who sign the cheques – the acid test of commitment to a cause. We shall see that the respectable and questionable motivations for archaeological work are closely related to the history of each country, and the present political and religious beliefs of its leaders. Readers must judge for themselves which of my thirteen motivations is present in each case.

Archaeology in **IRELAND** is supported by the state and the universities, and tends to be nationalist in both cases. Archaeology at University College, Dublin, is taught by a Department of *Celtic* Archaeology. Up to a point the Republic has encouraged the pursuit of Irish Archaeology, that is to say *real* Irish archaeology, by which they meant pre-Viking . The Irish coinage is based on symbols of their early culture (wolfhound, bear, harp, etc.) In Dublin the internationally important excavations of the rich Viking urban levels were starved of resources; much that was bulldozed away was as archaeologically rich and well preserved as the famous Viking dig of Coppergate in York. The director, Brendan Ó'Riordáin, appealed for more funds to his employers, the National Museum. The reply, with a sad smile, was 'Ah now, if only it were Early Christian!' Much passion and rancour was generated by later legal battles, resulting in a bout of fisticuffs outside the court between two very eminent archaeologists, one Irish, the other English.

These biases are also responsible for the concentration in Irish archaeology on what the late Michael O'Kelly (Professor of Archaeology at the University of Cork) used to call 'all those squiggles'. 'Squiggle archaeology' was concerned with Irish Christian art – high crosses, religious and other remains of Ireland's Golden Age. The discovery by a metal-detector, illicitly digging on an Irish monastic site, of the Derrynaflan Early Christian treasure, was hailed by the National Museum (but not by other responsible people in Ireland) as a great and important discovery for the nation. Academic life does not escape current politics in the secular sphere. Peter Fowler (then of the University of Bristol) and I gave papers in 1972 at a prestigious Irish conference, but had to leave a reception hastily when the president of the sponsoring academic organization said in a loud voice that 'the only Englishmen whom he could tolerate were those through whom he could see daylight;' we retreated from a fight on that occasion.

Much has been written on the use by the Nazis in **GERMANY** of Gustav Kossina's assumption of German racial purity and superiority. Not only were spurious racial ideas of Aryanism and Pan-German Nordicism perpetrated, but the chronology of German prehistory was (as Graham Clark puts it) 'so inflated that any innovation could be ascribed to a German origin, and its diffusion due to the dominance by Germans of inferior peoples, notably the Slavs.' (Kossina's theory has since been discredited – see Renfrew, 1973.) 'From Germany spread megalithic cultures of Indo-Germans; flint daggers were glorified as evidence of a noble pride and joy in weapons; the trumpets of the Nordic Bronze Age were evidence of German superiority in music already in prehistoric times, contrasting their majestic volume combined with gentleness with the monotone diatonic melodies of the south' (Clark, 1965, page 260). German archaeology has fortunately totally recovered its high position in European archaeology, with very large and efficient excavations and scholarship of the highest academic standard. Some of the most important work in Germany has been in on the early medieval period. This is because this was one of the high points of German civilization; the fifth and sixth centuries are when German culture was exported (at sword-point) to revitalize the decadent Latin culture of the Roman Empire (and hence the English!).

Each country takes pride in its Golden Age, and this is reflected in its archaeology and museum display. In **SCANDINAVIA** the Swedes show the rich remains of their seventh-century Vendel and Valsgärde cultures, pre-Viking and contemporary with Sutton Hoo (Chapter 8). The Norwegians, on the other hand, are proud of their Viking past. At Oslo there is a magnificent ship-museum of this age, and it was of course a Norwegian who sailed a Viking replica ship across the Atlantic in 1893; it was a Norwegian who, in 1978, with his 13-year-old daughter, rowed across the North Sea, and up the River Ouse to York, possibly to reclaim the lost kingdom of Eric Blood-Axe. Denmark has enormous public support for archaeology. Its popular magazine, *Skalk,* has a circulation of over 50,000, forty times that of its English equivalent per head of the population. Their prehistory and Vikings are equally popular. It was their Bronze Age trumpets *(lurs)* which gave the name to *Lurpak* butter.

In the **NETHERLANDS** the Dutch destroyed much of their medieval heritage in their Golden Age of the seventeenth century, but we are left with the glories of the new work in places like Amsterdam, Leiden and Delft. Holland is one of the few places where, in the course of several tours, I have detected no motivation that was not of the most impeccable academic order, whether by state or university.

I have already mentioned **RUSSIA's** laudable attempt to stress the essential prehistoric unity of widely distant areas of the USSR. Nationalism, however, plays an important role in decision making in the financing of public archaeology. One of the longest drawn out disputes in the interpretation of archaeological finds centres on the area around Lake Ladoga. Here there are rich cemeteries with Swedish-made swords. To the Swedes, these are evidence of the graves of aristocratic or entrepreneurial merchants who had penetrated the river-systems. These merchants, the *Rus* or Eastern Vikings, went on eventually to the glories of Byzantium, and their enrolment in the crack Varangian Guard there. To the Russians, however, these weapons belonged to the indigenous Slavic people, who by means of *their* mercantile genius, had developed the economy, markets and wealth and made them able to buy this prestigious equipment.

It was nationalism too which led to the financing of massive excavations in Novgorod, dear to Russian hearts as the predecessor of Moscow before the fifteenth century, and the symbol of 'old Mother Russia'.

A major issue beyond the scope of this book (i.e. the author's competence) is the extent to which political ideologies affect not just the financing of archaeology, but also the ultimate interpretation of the results; in this case this is heavily linked to Marxism, a system of explanation and indeed motivation which has many repercussions in the archaeological theory of countries outside Russia, including Britain.

We know very little of the important archaeology of **CHINA.** For a long time it was the preserve of foreign scholars, who experienced difficulties. Archaeology was, in the peasants' view, unpropitious, 'jarring the susceptibilities of the spirits and interfering with fertility' (Clark, 1965, page 258). After the revolution, archaeology was taken up in a big way by the communist state as a major tool in inculcating pride, not only in China's past, but in the earlier achievements of the workers.

A major revelation in Britain was the 'Genius of China' Exhibition, displayed at the Royal Academy in London in 1973–74. There was a dazzling display of treasure of superb artistic quality, including the famous suit for the corpse of a princess, made of jade plaques. The message of the text of the guide, in spite of some editing in translation, came through loud and clear. There was primacy of invention (notably of metal-working); but what was most impressive was the justification for the excavation of rich aristocratic tombs rather than prehistoric peasant settlements. 'These amazing finds', ran the blurb, 'were made by the ordinary people, the artisans, working for their effete lords. Now they are being excavated and restored to the Chinese people who made them' (i.e. by display in the Museums of the Chinese People's Republic), a valid point, I feel.

Fagan (1978) supplies further telling quotes from Chinese publications. 'Archaeology is used to underscore the suffering of workers in pre-revolutionary society.' 'Textile imports found in ancient cemeteries are evidence that China has always been interested in friendly Chinese neighbours.' 'The archaeological work at Lui Sheng's tomb of c.113 BC . . . has mercilessly expressed the limits and extravagance of the aristocrats, as well as their brutal exploitation and oppression of the workers.' 'Her suits had 2690 pieces of jade and 38,025 length of gold thread; all that remained of Lui Sheng were teeth' . . . 'by destroying their bodies, history has exacted a just retribution.' 'Lady Tai . . . died of heart failure and gallstones . . . she was well-nourished, with much subcutaneous fat.' 'She had led', said the doctor, 'the idle dissipated life of the exploiting class.' As Chairman Mao said, 'let the past serve the present.'

All emergent nations, shaking off the shackles of imperialist domination, have used archaeology to develop and strengthen ancient roots and establish the new state on a consciousness of the great past. **INDIA** developed her own archaeology, staffed by Indians. Mortimer Wheeler, the great British archaeologist, went out in 1945 as Director General of Antiquities to train them in modern methods. **GHANA** took its name from a medieval state further inland which is not even in the area of the new state (it is what is now Mali). The most remarkable example is **ZIMBABWE.** The name is that of a remarkable site where there are seven square kilometres of extensive and massive stone buildings, witness to a very well-organized and technically competent earlier society. White racial prejudice would not allow that Great Zimbabwe had been built by indigenous Africans; it must have been the work of whites, whose identity ranged from the Queen of Sheba to early Portuguese merchants. It was, however, the work of white archaeologists less hostile to black aspirations which demonstrated beyond doubt that the site was earlier than European influence, and that its material culture was wholly indigenous. This demonstration of a former greatness made Zimbabwe the symbol of the new country and gave it its 1980 name, helped by the fact that Robert Mugabe came from that area. The ruins have now been 'reclaimed' by local people who leave offerings of goats and meat on the site (BBC talk, 1983). Other monuments such as the European forts are being 'de-proclaimed' as ancient sites, since they are, according to the African spokesman, 'blatantly colonial – monuments of conquest'.

While African monuments such as Great Zimbabwe have become symbols of national identity, this very desire for nationhood is not consistent with the preservation of the local cultural heritage. Peter Ucko, now Professor of Archaeology at Southampton, was invited by the British Council to 'evaluate cultural awareness' in different parts of Zimbabwe, and assess the viability of developing a kind of museum to be called 'local culture houses'. These would attempt to preserve the material cultural heritage of local ethnic, linguistic or cultural groups. Objects of special value, including especially items of spiritual or 'ritual' significance would be in a locked room, but there would be more open areas with examples of arts and crafts (with direct sales to purchasers of items currently being made), taped oral histories and autobiographies.

While local peoples were strongly in favour of the development of culture houses, Ucko's report met with no support from the Zimbabwe government: 'archaeology could not be allowed to fuel the fires of potential rebellion'; the proposals smacked of 'tribalism' – a dirty word in an emergent nation. 'We must lose our ethnic identities in order to find our true selves within the context of Zimbabwean identity;' 'by the time our children leave secondary school, they should simply regard themselves as Zimbabweans irrespective of their tribal, regional or racial origins' (quotations from two Zimbabwe newspapers in May/June, 1981). Ucko's report was suppressed by both the British Council *and* by the Zimbabwe government, and it was never published.

One major problem in African archaeology is to persuade Africans to be their own archaeologists. In emergent nations educated young people seek a higher status in society such as that afforded by being a lawyer.

Nationalism is also a major factor in developing the archaeology of any nation which has a 'glorious' past. In **ITALY**, the Roman past hardly needed stressing: Rome is substantially Roman. Mussolini, however, capitalized on this, pouring money into the uncovering of more and more monuments, and adopting the symbol of the *fasces* as his own. This was the symbol of the *lictors,* the chief Roman officials of law and order, and hence, for Mussolini, it became the symbol of order, discipline, and authority, as much as of Rome itself. *Senatus populusque Romanus* finds its echo in the SPQR on manhole covers and other public utilities in Rome (these are coveted by my son, whose names are Sebastian Patrick Quintus!). Italy also provides us with an example of 'religious' archaeology. The Vatican sponsored excavations under St Peter's in the hope of discovering the tomb of St Peter; not surprisingly the published work leans over heavily to a positive interpretation of the results. Credibility would have been higher if the archaeologists responsible for the work had not been Roman Catholic priests.

Religion and nationalism came together in **ISRAEL**. It was a military commando who was also an archaeologist, Yigael Yadin, who was given enormous resources to dig Masada, the scene of the self-immolation of the Jews under Roman government. The rocky fortress is a patent symbol of Zionism today. Moshe Dayan, another Israeli leader, expressed his belief in the purpose of archaeology succinctly: 'It is so I understand my people and feel proud.' In neighbouring **JORDAN**, the government looks back to its Roman past, to the cities of the Decapolis. Large government-sponsored excavations at sites such as Jerash are undertaken by archaeologists recruited from several countries. Recently Crown Prince Hassan of Jordan (on BBC Chronicle, 1983) emphasized the role of Jerash as 'a cultural contribution to the psychology and morale of the Jordanian people'.

In **YUGOSLAVIA**, Tito also had the task of merging diverse ethnic and cultural groups into a single state. Archaeology has not, however, been used for this purpose: the main motive in sponsoring excavations is financial – the promotion of tourism. In 1972 I worked on an American/Yugoslav excavation on Diocletian's Palace at Split. The whole aim was not the understanding of the palace's remarkable urban continuity from the fourth century to the present day. Medieval levels were swept away, the object being to uncover Roman structures and mosaics and rich finds. The structures uncovered were rapidly consolidated and incorporated into new cafés. Hundreds of tons of stratified archaeological deposits were removed from the deep cellar-basements of the palace to allow them to be opened to public view. The 'dirt' was passed out along conveyor belts; anything 'important' such as statues, was picked off, and the rest was dumped in the sea.

Archaeology in Islamic countries is geared to the Islamic revolution. In **IRAN**, non-Islamic (Persian) monuments were severely damaged in the early excesses of the revolution. In **LIBYA**, Colonel Ghadafi is personally interested in archaeology – of a certain kind. In 1978 I was invited to take over the excavations at Surt, a coastal town in the Libyan Gulf. This is a place of early medieval origin, not Roman, and as such owed its early importance to the growth of Islam as a trading centre of the Eastern Mediterranean. I expressed an interest, keen to extend my urban and cultural experience, and involve my department in Mediterranean medieval archaeology. A research strategy was devised which would examine the town and its hinterland in a way which would define its natural resources, its origins, its town plan, the functions of its different areas, its trading connections and its economy – all standard objectives in modern urban studies. We were, however, over-optimistic in believing that the results would be of great interest to a modern Islamic state interested in its past. Ghadafi made his objections very clear. He was not interested in such a theoretical approach; what he wanted was someone who could uncover mosques, mosaics, and recover fine glass and ceramics which would, in his view, redound more to the glory of Islam than to the aims of modern archaeology.

In **MOROCCO**, the great monuments of Islam, the palaces, mausolea, and mosques of the former dynasties, are religious monuments, which are visited by Europeans as a tourist concession. Moulay-Idriss was the nucleus of Islamic political and military conquest of the area (hence its proximity to the former Roman city, now the ruins, of Volubilis). In the eighth century, however, it became the centre for the Islamic faith. From then on, its political importance waned in favour of Fez, Rabat, Meknes and other dynastic centres, and it became a holy city, the 'poor man's Mecca' for those whose resources did not allow the long trek to Saudi Arabia. Since the modern Islamic revolution, Moulay-Idriss is closed at times to non-Islamic tourists. One has to go to Spain to see Islamic monuments in all their glory, as secular tourist attractions, at Granada or Córdoba.

Independence movements can also seek the support of archaeology in rather curious ways. That in the **CANARIES**, although instigated by secessionist Spaniards, has as its graffito-message, *Guanche Indepencia*. The Guanche were the indigenous inhabitants of the Canaries, probably of Berber origin, who are represented in archaeology by stone tools, rock-paintings and tombs. They put up a surprising and long drawn out resistance to Iberian *conquistadores*.

In the past, archaeologists, along with soldiers, merchants, missionaries and anthropologists, were the agents and supporters of colonial oppression studying 'primitive' peoples as inferior to whites, but possibly as throwing some light on the life of our own 'barbarous' ancestors. Anthropologists have learnt their lesson here and abandoned their patronizing stance. In order to study other living societies, they have to adopt a posture of 'we are here to learn from you – our society is decadent and we have valuable lessons to learn.' They have also to bear with with the inhabitants' aspirations of becoming westernized (oddly, the indigenes don't believe all these stories about how awful life is in the USA or Western Europe), and in the process they see them lose those cultural characteristics which make them an invaluable source for the study of men. The people also demand a share in the profits of any book or film which may be made of their activities. Anthropologists are now, together with archaeologists, firm anti-imperialists; as we have already seen in the case of Zimbabwe, the latter can provide valuable ammunition in the fight for independence. They can show, for instance, that Indians in the USA or Aborigines in Australia have occupied the land for very long periods of up to 40,000 years or more. This destroyed the claims of white colonialists that the indigenous people had not been there very long and that dispossession was wholly justified in terms of developing resources. Archaeologists can show the antiquity not only of man, in those areas, but of cultural and ethnic groupings; and notably the antiquity of cemeteries. Their evidence has become increasingly important in re-establishing rights to land, and in re-ratifying former treaties.

Archaeologists have made direct contributions to the development of Third World countries by the improvement of living standards. Jean Gimpel has attempted to reintroduce simple 'lost technologies'; advanced machinery imported from the West is unsuitable because cost and maintenance requirements exceed local skills and reserves. For instance the simple horizontal-wheeled watermill (one of my own areas of research – Chapter 6) is being introduced into India and Africa by means of scale model demonstrations. In South America, Inca irrigation systems have been excavated and re-used.

In Northern **CANADA**, the indigenous Inuit Eskimos came into conflict with modern developers who wanted to build a large hydro-electric complex (*The Times*, 20th February, 1982). This would have had a deleterious effect on their traditional hunting and fishing territories. The Inuits and Crees, assisted by sympathetic Canadians, stopped the project. A year later, an agreement was signed by all parties, making sure that future projects took all ecological needs into account. A seven-year World Wildlife Fund research worked out harvest needs and total food inputs of the Eskimos. This study is of great interest in demonstrating to archaeologists possible factors to take into account when interpreting the life of early hunter–gatherers in the north.

In modern **AUSTRALIA**, sometimes known as the 'fourth world', the aborigine has all but lost his former way of life. For long despised as 'abbos', these indigenous people fell victim to exploitation, degradation, and extermination. Archaeology has shown that they can claim to be the most successful human beings in the world, having achieved a stable and balanced society in a hostile environment for forty millennia. Not many Australians believe this. When I expounded this view to a highly educated Australian post-graduate at York, her face exhibited utmost horror at this heresy. She gasped out, 'but they're just *animals*', and our conversation closed.

Some anthropological work was done in Australia in the postwar decades but, in common with all such researches, little attention was paid to material culture; emphasis was on societal institutions, kinship, inheritance and other related topics. It was only in 1972 that archaeologists began to record the technical aspects of aboriginal culture. Some aborigines have tried to return to their former lifestyle by going into the outback. They did not wish to relinquish wholly the efficient tools of the whites. Apart from steel knives and rifles, they wanted to take with them tape-recorders. This they saw as an invaluable way not only of recording their folklore from an ever-diminishing number of old people, but of making sure it would never again be lost. Other aborigines have been to the Ethnographic Museum at Sydney to find out the uses of various tools, and the meaning of symbols. The archae-ological director, Ronald Lampert, is increasingly a source of enlightenment to aborigines seeking to re-establish their cultural identity, and has not surprisingly become a champion of their aspirations to recover their lost status. Lampert and other archaeologists have also been involved in saving important aboriginal sacred sites from flooding (by the proposed Tasmanian dam), exploitation or tourism. It was an encouraging victory when Ayres Rock was recently restored to the aborigines as one of their most important religious sites. Archaeological work of a high order on the part of academics of Sydney and Canberra has shown the antiquity of the aborigine, but too late to save him.

This might sound as if the archaeologists were the friends of the aborigine. This is what the white archaeologists may have felt or intended, but that is not the way that they appeared to the aborigine. Peter Ucko describes how they burst into tears when they see archaeologists at work, because of the disturbance of the natural world, created by their ancestors. Archaeologists were seen as 'disturbers of peace and religion'. They were 'the whites who dig holes that don't produce out of them either water or minerals which will bring us royalties'. Especially abhorrent to the aborigine is the excavation of human remains: 'the archaeologists are the whites who disturb our ancestors to show we've been here for 40,000 years, but we know already, we've always been here since the dreamtime.' They are neither impressed by, nor interested in, radio-carbon dating.

This opposition had reached such a pitch by the mid-1970s that archaeology was virtually at a standstill. In 1976, however, the situation was reversed when the new Land Rights Act enabled the aborigine to lay claim to land if he could show that 'he belonged there, owned it, and by kinship had always been there.' Archaeologists and anthropologists ceased to be the enemy, because they alone could (in theory) prove this longevity of occupation. Relationships changed from confrontation (sometimes at gun-point) to collaboration; by a *political* circumstance, archaeology was saved.

Another problem in Australian archaeology has been the definition and preservation of pre-colonial monuments. To the aborigines, the important places may be natural features such as Ayres Rock, or particular localities. These are important to them as places to keep free of modern development (and from the taints of tourism). This cuts little ice with the whites, however, who can only see ancient monuments as things made by human beings which you can go and gape at. In Australia, this means especially rock-paintings, which may date from many thousands of years ago, or from more recent times. Australian governments, by attempting to preserve these, are imposing their own cultural viewpoint on the need to preserve the heritage, taking little notice of the interests of the indigenous minority. This now numbers between a quarter and half a million, depending on how an aborigine is defined, or 1–2 per cent of the total population. Many aborigines live in cities, and have vehicles, guns and other 'amenities' of white life. The only benefit they get from the preservation of rock-paintings are the profits of tourist exploitation, where they can, with the help of the archaeologist, lay a claim to ownership.

Attempts have been made to 'educate' the aborigine into an understanding of his own archaeology in scientific rather than dreamtime terms. They are increasingly represented on committees concerned with their own affairs, and offered help in attempts to preserve their cultural heritage for posterity. On hearing of these opportunities, an 84-year-old man applied to be taught how to dive. One of his ancestors had in dreamtime walked on the water across a strait; his footprints were believed to be preserved in the seabed, and the aborigine wished to record them for posterity.

Australia is an excellent example of the problems of studying the past of people who are still around. While intelligent consideration of their interests and grasp of their culture may vastly increase our understanding of their archaeology, white archaeologists have until recently treated pre-colonial archaeology as if it were that of a dead people, as we do in Europe. In terms of social relevance, the fruits of archaeology are for the benefit of the wider public. In Australia there must surely be especial consideration given to providing the aborigine with an archaeology not based on Europa-centric concepts, but with one appropriate to his interests. It is no use expounding cultural sequences and radio-carbon datings to a people who have only two kinds of time, the 'moving present' (extending back within living memory and extending into the near future) and 'ancestral time', the whole of the remote past; or attempting to speak of 'aboriginal archaeology' to an indigenous minority who even now (though not for long) have 200 separate languages with different vocabularies and different grammars.

I am indebted to Peter Ucko for most of the material in the above section. He was highly influential in attempting to secure adequate consideration of the cultural interests of the aborigine when he was Director of the Australian Insitute of Aboriginal Studies. This is a body which researches aboriginal research in linguistics, psychology, anthropology, and human biology as well as archaeology. It may well be, he suggests, that we are being equally arrogant in our attempts to promote our scientifically-based archaeology to our own white contemporaries. Even in England the majority of people have no conception of a past measured in millennia and centuries.

Similar problems exist in **NEW ZEALAND**: here archaeological remains, are (apart from 'historical' European sites of the eighteenth and nineteenth centuries) of only one culture, the Maori. They are also of relatively recent date, New Zealand having been colonized from Polynesia only about a thousand years ago. When the first settlers found a fauna wholly unused to human predators, life was easy. Maori archaeology is of the greatest interest; earthworks and settlement sites abound, including lots of hillforts similar to those of our own European Iron Age. European scholars, such as Lady Aileen Fox, have taken a keen interest in their archaeology.

Here also there have been similar clashes of interests concerning ownership of sacred areas of land, and attempts to preserve Maori culture and language. Far from being a potentially dying indigenous minority, Maoris, after being decimated by white exploitation and disease, have recently doubled in number and have become highly vociferous and politically effective in securing their legal rights. They want nothing less than a bi-cultural and bi-lingual society, with Europeans learning Maori. The indigenous cultural heritage (here, however, no more than a millennium old) is clearly in safe hands, and it will be interesting to see how this affects Maori achaeology, and their own participation in their past (BBC, *The World About Us,* 23rd March, 1984). A full understanding of Maori archaeology does demand a full integration of surviving folklore, ethnography, and traditional history. The Maori are understandably reluctant to divulge all their secrets and religious beliefs. It is said that in order to study Maori archaeology properly, one has to marry a Maori – a radical step which Aileen Fox has not yet taken.

We may next look at the **UNITED STATES OF AMERICA**. Many of the most influential ideas and theoretical approaches of modern archaeology have originated there in the last decade or two. They have arisen from two strangely contrasting aspects of North American archaeology which illustrate something of their philosophy. Firstly we consider the archaeology of the indigenous Indian. Indian culture and most of the people having been destroyed in ways which are remarkably familiar to us from hundreds of films, and degraded into tourist-souvenir reservations, Indians have recently begun to be the subject of theoretical study.

Their monuments get little better shrift. In New York state, I photographed two plaques which were meant to draw the public's attention to 'archaeological' monuments. One, close to an Indian settlement, is in the form of a white Christian cross, with a metal plate which reads:

GANNAGARD

Largest of the Genesa Indian villages, was located on Boughton Hill. Rev J. . . . C. . . . preached and baptised here in 1677. The place was also visited by Rev J. . . . G. . . . and other Jesuit Missionaries. Rev J. . . . G. . . . had chapel and resided here in 1676–1677.

The place was destroyed by de Nonville's army in 1687 and the inhabitants driven eastwards towards . . . and Geneva.

I was warned not to attempt to look at the site of the village, as there was a rather unfriendly Indian living there who had a shotgun!

Another plaque, in the small town of Victor nearby was

made of metal. Surmounting it was a low relief depiction of an Indian Chief complete with archetypal headdress, and a Christian cross hung round his neck. The text below ran:

In Perpetuation of the name of
ATHASATA (KRYN)

The Great Christian Mohawk Chief, Promoter of Peace, respecter of treaties, defender of righteousness, valiant warrior, leader of Indian forces forming one-third of the army of the de Nonville expedition, which *passed* (1687) *along the Indian trail*. [my italics]

'I cannot speak too highly of the assistance we received from the great Mohawk and his warriors: Our Christian Indians surpassed all, and performed deeds of valor, especially the Iroquois, upon which we had not dared to rely to fight against their relatives'. (De Nonville)

The name of ATHASATA merits a place in history beside the great Iroquois leaders.

– and we might add, alongside notable traitors elsewhere. What is surprising about these notices is that they were erected in relatively modern times, but do not appear to be embarrassing to the present community.

Fortunately, the tide is turning. The present generation of younger 'enlightened' American archaeologists *is* interested in the Indians, not only as a series of remarkable groups in themselves, but also in their aspirations to social justice. As in Australia, the demonstration by archaeologists of the 40,000-year antiquity of the Indian, and of his use of local resources over very long periods, has done much to offset claims that the 'recently-arrived' Indians had no better claim to the land and minerals than the invading whites. Archaeological evidence is brought to bear in law courts in support of modern Indians' claims to land and the honouring of long-dishonoured treaties.

American whites do of course, suffer from an inferiority complex about the slight antiquity of their culture. Some seek desperately to show that America was visited or even colonized long before Columbus (see Chapter 7). Others are inspired by nationalism to study the times of the pioneer settlements and the revolution, the war against the British. This is their historical archaeology – the excavation, and study from documents, of eighteenth and nineteenth century frontier forts, trading stations, and early towns such as Williamsburg. To us this seems all a bit recent, but not to Americans. The work in this field is, however, of the greatest interest, not only because of the opportunity to relate surviving material culture to plentiful written sources, but because of the use made of this data by New World archaeologists to develop archaeological theory.

These are wholly academic studies of a high order, yet they also serve a nationalistic sentiment. The 'ancient monuments' of Boston are the 'freedom trail' – the places where Bostonians rebelled against the English, culminating in the 'tea party'. At Marblehead, Massachusetts, the 'Old Burial Hill', where there is a fine collection of early gravestones, is marked by a plaque:

1630–1930

Established in 1638, one of the oldest graveyards in New England, Site of first meeting-house, *Six hundred revolutionary heroes* and several early pastors were interred at the top of the hill. [my italics]

It is the revolution, rather than the early settlers, which is the dominant attraction of this archaeology.

After this whirlwind and superficial tour of other countries' archaeology, we may ask whether the motivation for British archaeology is equally various or dubious ethically, and this is the subject of our next chapter.

3

British Archaeology

What of British archaeology? Is it all geared to academic research of a disinterested kind, free from all taint of political bias, or other distortions of the truth for non-scholarly ends? Not quite, I fear. Among the motivations listed above we appear on the whole to be free of any attempt to give priority to nationalist interests. King Arthur is an interesting example. If he existed as a historical figure at all, it was as a champion of the Christian British (in the dark age following the end of Roman Britain), against the threat of incoming English (Anglo-Saxon) immigrants. But in the twelfth century we find him as a popular folk-hero of the British, by that time Welsh and English together. Today, at the popular level, Arthur has a major following, and gets as much press as the thoroughly English cake-burner Alfred, though the two are conflated in the popular mind, as 'in 1066 and all that' where the paragraph on the famous cakes alternates Arthur and Alfred as the one responsible – here as a national hero opposing the Vikings.

Indigenous prehistory is accorded no more public or academic support than the archaeology of the wholly alien Romans, though Boudicca, the Iron Age queen who revolted against Roman rule, is another popular heroine. The British west of the 'Dark Ages' is studied with its early Anglo-Saxon (enemy) counterpart in the east. Anglo-Saxon Sutton Hoo (Chapter 8) is a prestige project, but so too is Viking York.

The invading Normans stimulate extensive studies of their castles and churches.

On the other hand one of the most costly recent operations, the lifting from the seabed of the wreck of Henry VIII's battleship, the *Mary Rose*, was undoubtedly helped by nationalist feeling that Britain was 'great' in those golden Tudor days. And to go back a little earlier, the inaugural lecture given by one of the most eminent of British Anglo-Saxon scholars, the late Dorothy Whitelock, was very much a glorification of all things Anglo-Saxon, as too was much of earlier nineteenth century attitudes to our early Anglo-Saxon material (cf. Horsman, 1976, and White, 1971).

Wales and Scotland do of course have nationalistic aspirations to self-government. In archaeology, this is reflected in the museums, in the sense that they display local material, such as that in the National Museum of Wales. A BBC TV play, 'The Extremists', whose theme was Welsh nationalism, began and ended with scenes of an archaeologist, the implication being that archaeology would naturally be demonstrating Wales' pre-English past. Academically, there is of course the Board of Celtic Studies; when I gave the O'Donnell Lecture in Welsh Universities in 1980 (Rahtz, 1982), it had, like all this series, to be concerned with Celtic peoples in Wales or overseas.

In contrast to this mainly even-handed interest in Britain's own past, some British archaeological resources are directed extensively to the past of *other* countries. Many academic archaeologists do field research in other countries, increasingly to the annoyance of their inhabitants. Even in Wales, the excavation hut of an English archaeologist was daubed 'English Go Home'.

Figure 3 shows the outline of a Roman fort in the university campus at Birmingham which was largely destroyed without excavation by the university's own buildings and car-parks, while its archaeologists were directing their research elsewhere. Such digging as was possible was done instead by the Birmingham Achaeological Society. This is a kind of inverse snobbery, the belief (shared to some extent by major archaeologists such as Mortimer Wheeler), that somehow Britain

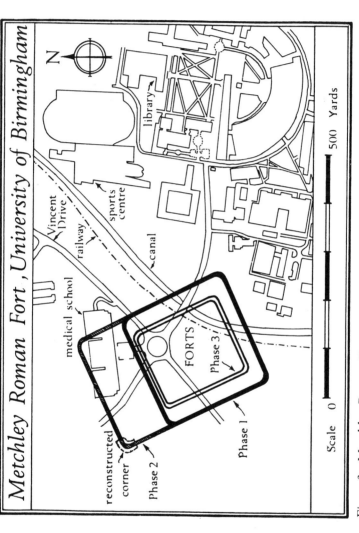

Figure 3 Metchley Roman Fort, University of Birmingham.

is a bit peripheral, compared to the 'great civilizations' of Rome, Greece or the Near East. This view has been considerably modified in recent years by the advent of absolute dating, such as that from radio-carbon. This shows that some of our major prehistoric monuments, such as megalithic tombs, are actually earlier than the eastern Mediterranean 'prototypes' from which they were supposedly derived by the process of 'invasion' or 'diffusion' – two explanations of culture change that have gone out of fashion in recent years.

TOURISM AND THE CULTURAL HERITAGE*

Archaeology is used in England for public education, through tourism, centred on archaeological sites and monuments, national parks, and museums. The 'cultural heritage syndrome' – the enlightenment of people about their past – is one of the chief planks on which archaeologists in this country try to get funds from central or local government. At Bordesley Abbey, our excavations provide an 'ancient monument' for the New Town of Redditch, giving new immigrants some roots in a sense of history.

We have had, until recently, an excellent record in public education through our 'ancient monuments'. They have been well cared for and displayed, at considerable public expense, by what was until recently the relevant branch of the Department of the Environment. Gate receipts were low, except for such popular sites as Stonehenge (where the associated archaeological evidence was in danger of being worn away by visitors' feet). This was partly because the general public did not understand the monuments: a chunk of ruined masonry labelled 'reredorter' is not very evocative unless the tourist is versed in medieval monastic architecture and space-function.

There has accordingly been a trend in the last few years not only to 'liven up' our monuments and make them more educational at a lower level, but also to make money out of them by 'privatization'. The model here was the exploitation

*See also Chapter 9.

of 'historic houses' by their blue-blooded owners. There was a (fortunately erroneous) rumour that lions were to be introduced into Fountains Abbey, a magnificent Cistercian ruin in Yorkshire. The Conservative government of the early 1980s scrapped the older framework concerned with ancient monuments and a new semi-autonomous Historic Buildings and Monuments Commission was set up. Significantly its first chairman is Lord Montagu of Beaulieu, one of those very aristocrats who had commercialized their ancestral homes in order to survive. The outcome may not be so grim for archaeology as some fear – there are two highly reputable academic archaeologists on the Commission – but clearly tourism and financial profit must not gain at the expense of a purely academic or educational approach.

RELIGION

Further down towards the 'dubious' end of the motivation scale are the promotion of religious truths (in this case Christianity) and even worse, the support of myth. The latter is such a big topic that it has been reserved for another chapter (Chapter 7). The former is worth examining briefly by a few examples, because the 'aspersions' I cast here are by no means supported by general academic opinion. The 'bending' of archaeological 'truth' is no more than a matter of being 'generous to the evidence' (a splendid euphemism in this context). The archaeologists concerned are moreover mostly scholars of a far higher order than myself, and considerable authorities in their field.

There is in Britain between the fourth and eighth centuries AD an overlap between the pagan beliefs of the Romans and early Anglo-Saxons, and the gradual spread (with some severe setbacks) of Christianity. The latter is either remnant from Romano-British times, the result of Irish missions, or those from Rome represented by such figures as Augustine and Paulinus, and described so well by Bede. The relevant archaeological sites of this period – cemeteries and temples/ churches – not surprisingly generate much academic discussion about their interpretation, whether pagan or Christian, or a mixture. It so happens that the archaeologists concerned (and indeed most of those who study undoubted *churches* and their surroundings) are themselves Christians. This has, perhaps understandably, caused them to lean towards a Christian interpretation of borderline cases which is not always fully warranted by the evidence. Two examples must here suffice.

Many graves in the later Roman period in Europe are orientated west–east (heads to west). These include many cemeteries which are undoubtedly non-Christian. This fashionable orientation was taken over by Christians (without any authority of Holy Writ) and is with us to this day, as is the similar orientation of churches. To infer, however, that a cemetery of west–east graves in (say) the sixth or seventh centuries is Christian, in the absence of an associated church, is quite unjustified, but is very common even in present-day academic archaeological writing.

My second example is Tintagel. For a long time the ruins on this splendid Cornish headland were believed to be 'King Arthur's Castle'. Indeed they are still called this locally. Tintagel village is rich in 'Halls of Chivalry', 'King Arthur's car-park', etc. Although the largest ruins on the headland are indeed those of a castle (though of medieval date, centuries later than Arthur), excavations in the 1930s and 1940s revealed a number of structures of a lesser order, and a great many finds. The latter are of the greatest interest. They include pieces of hundreds of pots which were made not in Cornwall, but in very far distant places in North Africa and the Eastern Mediterranean. There they can be dated firmly to the fifth–seventh centuries by coin evidence, and since the areas concerned were fully Christian by this time, some pieces exhibit as decoration Christian symbols – crosses, alpha/ omega, saints, etc. The trade or other mechanisms by which such pottery was imported into Britain are a matter of continuing debate. One interpretation, favoured by the excavator of Tintagel and by others, is that the pots were associated with Christian movement directly from those areas into Western Britain and Ireland. They are parts of *amphorae* (general-purpose containers) and table-ware. The 'Christian' interpretation was that they were for use in the Mass, the table-ware being for the Host, and the amphorae for the wines. The excavator interpreted the structures uncovered as those of a Celtic monastery, similar to early monastic sites in, for example, Egypt. This is what they are now labelled as on the site. There is however no evidence that would be accepted by modern 'rigorous' archaeologists that the pottery was associated with these structures at all. Current opinion is that the latter are medieval, and associated with the castle; and that the pottery is part of a big rubbish deposit from secular buildings of considerable importance in areas not yet excavated. The pottery would in this case be 'prestige' material associated with an important chief, or with a major administrative or trade centre. Perhaps after all King Arthur was nearer the mark – the pottery is at least of a suitable date!

THE JEWISH CEMETERY IN YORK
AND OTHER SKELETONS IN THE CUPBOARD

Another interesting example, of quite a different kind, of the effect of religion on archaeology in Britain, is provided by the excavation of the Jewish cemetery in York in 1983. York has a bad name, even today, with the Jewish Community, similar to that of Belsen or Auschwitz. This is because of the massacre of Jews in the castle tower there in 1190 (all Jews were expelled from Britain exactly a hundred years later, in 1290). There is good historical evidence that the Jews of York and other towns nearby were buried in an area in York called Jewbury. Accordingly, when in 1982 the area was sold for development as a car-park associated with a new Sainsbury's supermarket, the York Archaeological Trust pointed out the historical evidence, and the possibility of a large Jewish cemetery being encountered. Support was sought for excavation from both Sainsbury's and from the Jewish community, in the belief that it was better for the cemetery to be carefully (and decently) excavated by archaeologists, than to be churned up by bulldozers.

The Chief Rabbi in London (Sir Immanuel Jakobovits)

refused even to countenance the idea of a Jewish cemetery being disturbed; he did, however, support a proposal for an excavation to see whether burials were, in fact, present, provided that no bones were moved. A trial excavation in the threatened area did indeed reveal many graves, orientated north–south. There were nailed wooden coffins, of men, women and children, and of medieval date. Again the Chief Rabbi was approached, and the discoveries were considered by the Chief Rabbi's Court of Beth Din. The Court refused to believe that the graves found were those of Jews, who, it was said, were never buried north–south or with coffin nails; and no Jewish objects or tombstones had been found. In fact, the only evidence for the cemetery being Jewish was that of 'very old documents'. In effect they washed their hands of the whole matter.

Since the existence of a cemetery had now been proved, Sainsbury's were under a legal obligation, under an English law of 1981 (Disused Burial Grounds Amendment Act), to remove all skeletons from areas to be disturbed. Under the Home Office licence issued to them they undertook to rebury the remains 'without undue delay' in adjacent 'safe' ground. They contracted this work to the Archaeological Trust (rather than to professional 'cemetery-clearing' firms who do suprisingly exist). In the spring and summer of 1983 over 500 graves were excavated, a cemetery of the greatest interest to students of medieval burial practice, and to the study of medieval human skeletons. No archaeological evidence was in fact found for the cemetery being Jewish (what could there be, in the absence of grave memorials?); but the coincidence of a large medieval cemetery, with distinctive burial rites, not associated with any known church, and the historical evidence, left very little room for doubt that it was the Jewish Cemetery of York that had been excavated.

Work proceeded during the summer and autumn on the analysis of the results, and on the measurement of the bones, and on the search for any evidence of disease (such as arthritis or leprosy), or accident. This was done by human biologists at the University of York, with the aid of research funding provided by the Science and Engineering Research Council.

Interest generated a short account late in 1983 in the local newspaper, of 'Jews' skeletons being measured in York'; this was copied in the *Guardian*. Even though the Chief Rabbi disclaimed interest, a trainee rabbi and students of the orthodox Jewish College at Gateshead made a strong protest to him at the very concept of the measurement of Jewish skeletons being discussed in the public press – and in York of all places!

The Chief Rabbi may have had second thoughts about his earlier pronouncements, for he immediately complained to the Home Office. They, duly sensitive to the interests of religious minorities in Britain, ordered their representative in York, the local Environmental Health Officer, to order immediate reburial. Sainsbury's were asked to dig a hole for reburial and the University to give up the bones. Sainsbury's, the York Archaeological Trust, and the University of York all have a public image to maintain, so could hardly provoke a major scandal by refusing. Representations were, however, made to the Chief Rabbi and the Home Office, to give more time to complete the scientific examination.

In the event, a week's reprieve was granted before the bones were removed to a Jewish mortuary, to await reburial months later, but the biological examination was by no means complete, and the record is accordingly deficient. Members of the Jewish community from Manchester came to collect the bones from the University, and others from Gateshead came to make sure the whole process was carried out with reverence. The former group in fact expressed great interest in the biologists' findings; they could appreciate that the archaeologists had recovered evidence relevant to the history of the Jewish faith that would otherwise have been destroyed by Sainsbury's bulldozers; they described the research as 'fascinating'.

Each skeleton was placed in a separate heat-sealed poly-thene bag, with a plastic identity disc. These were then put in wooden boxes, which were removed in mid–December 1983. The Jews who collected these from the University hoped that it would be possible to re-inter them in the area of the new supermarket *in the same pattern as they had been excavated*, using the archaeologists' plan of the cemetery to achieve this end. To have carried this out would have needed a plot of land as large as that which the cemetery had formerly occupied, which just was not available in the crowded urban area of York. While negotiations proceeded on this point between the Jewish community and Sainsbury's, the bones were stored in the Jewish mortuary at Manchester.

The Jewish community wanted 300 rabbis to be present at the ceremony of re-interment, but Sainsbury's did not think it was possible to accommodate more than a few in the rather restricted area available. The bones were finally reburied on the same day as lightning destroyed the roof of the south transept of York Minster, from which we may draw our own conclusions!

This was not the first time that the Jews had objected to the disinterring of Jewish skeletons. A more serious case was that in Jerusalem in 1982, where there were near riots of protest against archaeologists excavating graves. This protest spread to Britain; a protest meeting was held in South Kensington by orthodox Jews protesting about the excavation of the ancient patriarchs; a photograph in *The Times* showed protestors at the meeting, holding up in their midst a skeleton, which we must presume was a plastic one used for medical teaching! Israeli law now lays down that no excavations may be made within half a mile of any known Jewish cemetery. Jewish objection to the excavation of graves by archaeologists is not, however, confined to those of Jews. A wider basis of protest, which is also shared by many non-Jewish people, is encapsulated in the following extract from a *Times* special article (11 January, 1984) by Bernard Levin (himself a Jew), which illustrates also how what began as a local archaeological problem in York had escalated to one of national and indeed universal interest:

IF THESE BONES LIE AT PEACE, CIVILIZATION CAN SURELY REST

There was a strange and little-remarked story the other day. . . . It concerned bones – 50,000 was the figure mentioned. . . . The bones came from graves which were believed to be those of Jews; . . . our century has seen Jewish bones produced in quantities never attained in all previous history, though . . . the massacre of Jews at York in the twelfth century had more than a touch of the murderous frenzy that raged in civilized Europe less than 50 years ago. The Chief Rabbi asked the archaeologists to cease work on the examination of the bones and rebury them where they had been found. His reason was 'the paramount concern for the reverence due to mortal remains which once bore the incomparable hallmark of the divine image, and which, we believe have an inalienable right to stay undisturbed'. He added that 'dignity shown to human remains, even centuries after death, could contribute more than any scientific inquiry to human civilization.' . . . Those bones may now sleep soundly, undisturbed by the trolleys of Sainsbury's customers, until they wake never to sleep again.

A final example of the potential disapproval of the disturbing of the dead by archaeologists refers to our own work at the medieval Cistercian Abbey of Bordesley, Redditch, near Birmingham. The source is the rather unexpected one of *Treasure Hunting* (November 1982), the magazine of the metal-detecting fraternity. They are here using *Roman Catholic* disapproval to back up their many-pronged attacks on establishment archaeology; this is the first time I have been described as a 'ghoul'.

ARCHAEOLOGICAL 'GHOULS' UNDER CRITICISM

The disturbing of the dead by archaeologists is yet again under criticism. This time a team of forty archaeologists (led by Professor Philip Rahtz) are interfering with 150 graves – some of them belonging to Catholic monks – on a dig being undertaken in the ruins of Bordesley Abbey.

Former Redditch police sergeant Richard Thornton-Pitt, himself a Catholic, has spoken out in condemnation. 'They shouldn't be interfering with these holy men buried in consecrated ground, it simply isn't right', he commented. 'How would they like it if someone dug their parents up?' Good for you, Mr Thornton-Pitt! This is not the first occasion on which local Catholics have had to stop archaeological grave-robbing. In 1967 Father Bede Moore presided over the reburial of a skeleton excavated from the Abbey cemetery 800 years after the original burial. 'It was decided he should be properly buried again rather than just becoming a souvenir piece', Father Bede commented.

INDIVIDUALS AND INSTITUTIONS

Much archaeology in Britain is motivated by the desire for self-aggrandizement of individuals or institutions; I have already mentioned this as the reason why I did and continue to do archaeology; it is my reason (apart from the fact that I like doing so) for writing this book. Such motivation is, however, normally concealed by a more respectable umbrella – I claim that I am writing this book to invite readers to become interested in archaeology, to educate them to want to know more, to promote a greater understanding in the cultured world about the framework within which archaeology works. All these are true to some extent, because it is by doing such things that I achieve or maintain status in society (hopefully not the reverse!) and satisfy my own intellectual and expressive needs. Similarly, when the British Museum hangs on to the Elgin marbles, it does not honestly admit that it wants to maintain its high status (as the place where the Elgin marbles may be seen) but builds up a complex justification based on London being a more convenient place for world scholars to see the marbles, a sort of international museum. Similar attempts at survival in society determine most archaeological work in Britain, though heavily and on the whole successfully disguised.

TREASURE-HUNTING

We need not dwell on the lowest of all motives for doing or promoting archaeology, that of treasure-hunting, profit, or looting. In Britain as elsewhere, there has been digging for cash, or saleable or convertible objects, since at least Roman times, often with high approval. The findspots are not properly recorded, and the finds themselves do not always reach museums where they can be studied or published. The situation has vastly deteriorated in recent years because of the extensive use of metal-detectors, and their high success rate. Most metal-detector users or clubs are merely ignorant of the evidence they destroy when they dig up a 'bleeped' find, but a hard core minority know only too well. They study archaeological publications to find out where to dig, and to find out what is valuable. They regard archaeologists as self-righteous spoilers of their pleasure and profit, when attempts are made by legislation or social pressure to restrict them. They are sometimes encouraged by land-owners or farmers in return for a 'cut', and it is even rumoured that some museums buy their finds, and advertise that they will. They justify this by saying that it is better for illicitly acquired items to find their way to museums rather than to dealers.

One such firm of antiquity dealers, Fox and Company, of Yeovil, Somerset, advertises finds from all over the world. Many are from Britain, usually given a vague location, such as 'North West Wiltshire'; or more specifically, Lamyatt, a temple site which suffered severely at the hands of local depredations. Three lead 'curses' (incised inscriptions on lead sheets, asking the gods to punish someone who has done wrong to the writer) were found by metal-detectors at the temple site of Pagans Hill, in Somerset, which I partly excavated in the 1950s. They were subsequently sold to Fox and Company who fortunately allowed them to be examined by experts, but of course I have no idea in what part of the site they were found, or at what depth.

This firm advertises on the back page of an English archaeological magazine, *Popular Archaeology*. This brought the magazine into some disrepute, and drew a letter to the editor in 1983 from '24 staff and research students at Cambridge'. They deplored the encouragement it appeared to give to those after financial gain; it would lead to further pillaging and loss of objects to dealers, and to archaeology being discredited.

To Fox's credit they reproduced the letter in their own magazine, the *Fox Review* (1982), which carries not ony lists of antiquities and books for sale, but also chatty articles about 'recent purchases' of British finds. The editor rather spoilt the impression of open-mindedness by a rather virulent and sarcastic attack on the Cambridge party. This example serves well to illustrate the nature of the currently bad relationships between archaeologists and treasure-hunters. All archaeologists like finding valuable or rare objects, and not only because they are very often also important evidence in the understanding of a site or period. This is only undesirable when their wish to find 'loot' determines the locality or strategy of excavation. Those who excavate and uncover many rich finds (such as the Roman temple at Uley, Gloucestershire) find it easier to get funds from museums (as happened in this case) for future work, in the expectation of further important finds accurring to the museum's collections. I was told by the editor of a county journal that their decision whether to publish my excavation report would be influenced by whether I deposited my finds in their county museum!

CONCLUSION

So Britain does have its non-academic reasons for the sponsoring or doing of archaeology. Each country has its own reasons for doing its own archaeology, dependent on its cultural and political history. Whatever the reasons, impeccably ethical or highly dubious, the work is done by archaeologists of varying integrity and quality. If all the archaeologists in the world were assembled together in a hugh international conference, what would they have in common? What would distinguish this interesting gathering from one of economists, politicians or statisticians? What special qualities does an archaeologist have to have? Is he born with a silver trowel in his hand, or does he acquire one by a cultural accident? These are questions now to be explored.

4

Who are the Archaeologists?

In discussing the various factors which combine to give birth to, or make, an archaeologist, we must restrict ourselves to those who have 'succeeded' in the subject; those who are either in full-time employment in university, museum, field unit, or public administration, or who are exceptionally talented amateurs. The latter, although they earn a living by doing something quite unrelated and futile like accountancy, are those who have made an important regional, national or international reputation by their work. Such a person was Leslie Grinsell who, while employed as a bank clerk, visited over 20,000 Bronze Age barrows in England, over a period of 20 years, and became the authority on them.

To be effective in archaeology, one has either to be a fairly low-level all-rounder like myself, who can do a reasonable job of excavating a site, publishing the results, doing some minor research, lecturing, travelling, writing or editing books, or training students; or a brilliant theorist, who may never go near a dig; or a synthesizer of other people's published work; or a specialist, such as someone who is the world's greatest authority on Roman wall-painting or Iron Age wheel-hubs.

It is always said there is a greater range among students with first-class degrees (bare firsts, good firsts, brilliant firsts, firsts of genius) than between them and the greater hosts of seconds and thirds. So too among archaeologists. The very

51

top class are those who have an international reputation and figure, or will figure in any textbook on the history of the subject. These are the Darwins or Einsteins of archaeology. Such were General Pitt-Rivers, the founder of modern scientific archaeology; Gordon Childe, the European prehistoric theorist; Mortimer Wheeler, perhaps the best known archaeologist ever, familiar alike to academic and lay public through TV; and, in our own day, Lewis Binford in the USA; and the late David Clarke at Cambridge. Such a list is highly invidious, and readers who are archaeologists are invited to compile their own select list.

In the second order are those who, while not having (as yet?) the universal world reputation of the above, have been highly effective in their own field, making crucial contributions. To list these would be even more invidious, and I am safer if I list only a few of those who are dead:

(1) Flinders Petrie, the Egyptologist
(2) Leonard Woolley, the excavator of Ur
(3) Abbé Breuil, the French Palaeolithic scholar
(4) Kathleen Kenyon, the excavator of Jericho
(5) Ian Richmond, the doyen of Roman Britain
(6) Eric Higgs, the Cambridge prehistorian
(7) Arthur Evans, the discoverer of Minoan Crete
(8) Michael O'Kelly, the greatest of all Irish archaeologists, and excavator of Newgrange.

Doubtless an American would have compiled a different list to my rather insular one. A third category would bring in many hundreds of names, past and present, but I hope I have now made my point about the rarity of top-notchers in what is, after all, a small professional subject compared with, say, history.

THE COMPLETE ARCHAEOLOGIST

Graham Clarke (1965) defined the 'complete archaeologist' as follows:

The complete archaeologist, if such a being existed, would need to have a genius for travel, exploration, and reconnaissance; to be adept at business and administration, skilled at raising funds and obtaining all manner of permits from authorities and owners, few of whom can hope to gain from his activities, and capable of administering and directing excavations which may well turn out to be large-scale enterprises; to be a competent surveyor, draughtsman, and photographer, so that what he finds can be adequately recorded; to combine a gift for exact description and analysis with a power of synthesis and a flair for journalism; and to have the gift of tongues, or at very least an ability to digest the reports of his foreign colleagues without which his own will lack the authority that only wide reading and comparison can provide

– a formidable list of attributes for any one person to possess. Not all are needed to be a successful archaeologist, in particular a specialist. What *all* archaeologists need are, not necessarily in this order, an intense interest in the past, or in the theory of archaeology, bordering on the fanatical; a capacity for sustained hard work, often in far from ideal conditions either in the field, library, or museum; high tolerance and acceptance of excruciating boredom; a lively but controlled sense of order, pattern, process and meaning; visual and conceptual imagination and a wide cultural perspective; and preferably, though not obligatory, an ability to communicate with other human beings in writing or speech. Since archaeology is about the whole past of human experience, it is especially useful to be a practical sort of person, knowing how things work, with some idea of how a farm is run, how a building is erected, or how the dead are disposed of.

How does one recognize these paragons in embryo? Is it possible to say, 'there goes the next David Clarke/Lewis Binford' when faced with a new intake of first-year students, of average age 18–19? I ask them, and myself, 'which of *you* are going to make it, at any level; which of you are going to be *doing* archaeology in ten years' time, and which of you will have given up and entered some other profession? To succeed in archaeology you have to *want to enough* (a very pregnant phrase); and you have to be *clever enough*; and you have to be in one way or another *lucky*. None of these is enough by itself.' I also tell them that in spite of current poor career prospects, I do not know of any really good archaeologist who is not in a job in archaeology of some kind, however grim or poorly paid; but that I know of many second-rate archaeologists in jobs who ought not to be employed at all!

How young does one have to start? Most first-year students have had little or no experience. Barry Cunliffe, now a professor of archaeology at Oxford, was, however, interested enough to be doing field-work before he was ten; Stuart Piggott (formerly professor of archaeology at Edinburgh) lectured to a Prehistoric Society field trip when he was 14 (but they didn't know that when they asked him!); Martin Biddle (who directed the great series of excavations at Winchester) and Lawrence Barfield (now at the University of Birmingham) were directing an important dig together while they were still at school; George Boon published his report of a major Roman villa excavation before he was 21; and many other examples can be found of such prodigies, which are rather off-putting to the average aspiring undergraduate.

What we need to know about archaeologists, to find out what makes them tick, is their family, genetic and cultural backgrounds; who or what influenced them in school or university; what opportunities came their way in later years, and how and why they responded to them in the way they did. Such data would be interesting in themselves in our current enquiry as to who is who and why, but also so that we may evaluate their published work in the light of all this. What biases are likely to be inherent in their approach (religious, Marxist, determinist, etc.) which may have to be allowed for? It has been suggested that archaeologists should psychoanalyse themselves at intervals throughout their life, so that they can either minimize bias, or be explicit about it in presenting a 'loaded' view.

Who are the Archaeologists?

Many professional archaeologists enter the field by a conventional route: interest in archaeology at school, first degree in archaeology, doctoral thesis, experience in field, academic or other post. Barry Cunliffe went through this mill, after his precocious start; he was a lecturer in his early twenties, and was appointed professor of archaeology at Southampton at the age of 26. A surprising number of the 'top 100' in British archaeology did not follow this path. Several did not go to a university at all (such as Professor Stuart Piggott and myself); many did first degrees in law, history, or science, and took up archaeology only as postgraduates. A few turned to it only in retirement. The most remarkable of these was Eric Higgs. He was a Shropshire sheep-farmer, with an amateur interest in palaeolithic archaeology. At the age of 56 he went to Cambridge as a student; later he was a research fellow and went on to be highly influential in early European prehistory; he initiated a new approach to archaeology based on a proper appreciation of the interaction of man with his environment.

There are not enough detailed biographies or autobiographies of archaeologists. When they do get written, they are usually full of academic interest and often highly colourful, such as Wheeler's own autobiography, or the more personal biography of him written by Jacquetta Hawkes, which treats of Wheeler's weakness for ladies as much as his talents as an archaeologist. I would appeal to archaeologists who read this book to write their autobiographies in fearless detail. They should write a first volume at the age of 40, and add to it each decade thereafter taking the opportunity to review and comment on what they had written earlier. These volumes would not necessarily be for publication (if they were honest, they would often be libellous or hurtful to the living) but as data for historians of archaeology in later times. Skinner, the early nineteenth century antiquarian and archaeologist, wrote nearly a hundred such volumes. When he died by his own hand in 1840, he left them to the British Museum with instructions to open them only in 1900. They are now a

55

major source for the social history and archaeology of his day, but one can see why he was reluctant for them to see the light of day while the objects of his acid remarks were still alive.

ONE MAN'S STORY

I have written part of my autobiography, starting it, however, too late when memory had faded (and worse, became selective). It is a difficult thing to be honest even with oneself; my experience has been that for an archaeologist at least, a thematic approach is likely to be more successful and useful than a chronological one, as long as there is some basic outline of events. While this is not the place for my autobiography, I end this chapter with a brief review of my career, including only those points that have a direct relevance to the themes of this book. It will serve as a case study of why and how one archaeologist proceeded on his way.

I was born in 1921, the last of five children. My father had a double first in English and Science and became an authority on English grammar and a schoolmaster. As children we were taken round on holidays to see castles, abbeys, museums and doubtless this sowed some seeds. I did classics at school, and do remember being intellectually excited (a rare thing – school to me was purgatory) by J.E. Barton, the headmaster, lecturing with slides on Mycenae. After a barely passed Matriculation, I'd had enough of learning, and left school at 16 to be articled to a chartered accountant. I quickly realized the essential immorality of this profession (making the rich richer). From all this I was saved by the Second World War.

I had been interested in archaeology in a minor way since I was a caver on the Mendip Hills, in North Somerset, in my teens. I became aware not only of the Mendip landscape of barrows and other earthworks, but also with the archaeology that was associated in that area very much with caves and cavers. The latter, in the course of digging to get down into cave systems often found archaeological material (cf. Wookey Hole and the Cheddar Caves). Indeed the two were combined academically in the University of Bristol Spelaeological

Society; this publishes both papers on scientific caving and on archaeology, in a journal to which I later contributed.

In the Royal Air Force I charged batteries, became an expert in the electrical side of radio-controlled bombs (the war alas ended just when we'd got the things working), but I also attended philosophy classes; and (perhaps most importantly for an archaeologist) learnt to put up with awful living conditions, and to 'get on' with the most unpleasant people I've ever met in my sheltered life. I ended up in 1944 as an education instructor, preparing airmen for return to civil life, teaching bookkeeping and current affairs. This was my start to a career in teaching and lecturing. More relevantly I was stationed on Salisbury Plain, near Stonehenge. Here I found myself in the next bed to Ernest Greenfield, a lifelong archaeologist who encouraged me, in our walks round the Plain, to develop my nascent interest in archaeology. My first archaeological 'lecture' was a 10-minute talk on the instructors' course, which was on the Mesolithic industries of Tardenois and the Mas d'Azil, culled from a popular textbook.

After the war, in 1946, I began digging on my own in Somerset, helped by advice from Greenfield and local archaeologists. This was not a job; I dug at weekends and holidays, helped by my wife and friends. I earned a precarious living as 'Studio Rahtz', a one-man business photographing babies, dogs and weddings. My first dig was what I thought was a Bronze Age barrow, but turned out to be a medieval windmill – perhaps prophetic of my later medieval interests. The second was a Roman temple at Pagans Hill, and this again had Saxon and medieval levels above it. By 1950 I'd got onto an emergency training scheme for schoolteachers (which I nearly failed) and I taught in secondary modern schools in Bristol from 1951 to 1953. This was even worse than *being* at school, and brought out unsuspected latent homicidal tendencies. My only escape was to take the boys digging at Pagans Hill.

By 1953, I had established a local reputation as an amateur digger, and it so happened that in that area a new reservoir was to be built. Here was the element of luck. Brian O'Neil, the then Chief Inspector of Ancient Monuments, asked me to cut a section across a Roman road that was to be flooded; I agreed, very flattered. The big surprises were (a) I'd have a *hut* to put tools in (b) I'd have *workmen* to do the digging, and – most gratifyingly – (c) I'd be *paid*. The job was to last two weeks, in the school holidays.

Figure 4 P. A. Rahtz Excavations, 1946–84.

Construction work began that Easter, and huge machines churned up the landscape. In an area of over 800 ha where no finds had ever been made, sites turned up all over the place – prehistoric, Roman and medieval. The work had to be extended, Greenfield (then unemployed) joined me, and I burnt my boats. I resigned from teaching to become a professional digger for the Inspectorate of Ancient Monuments and anybody else who would pay me.

This was a risky thing to do; we were paid only by the day, and there was none of the security that teaching offered; I had moreover by that time three children. I was, however, more interested in digging than in attending to the welfare of my family. I dug full time from 1953 to 1963, with some useful extramural teaching experience. I have dug Mesolithic, Neolithic, Bronze Age, Iron Age, Roman, Dark Age, Saxon, medieval and post-medieval sites in fourteen different English counties (figure 4) and in Ghana, Yugoslavia and Greece. I have had a wealth of practical experience in many different soils and types of site – caves, buildings, Roman roads, cemeteries, villas, temples, watermills, churches, monasteries, palaces, moated sites, towns, castles, hillforts and even a Norman tunnel. More importantly, I learnt how to draw and write, and to *publish* the results of excavations.

By 1963 when I applied for a lecturer's post at Birmingham, I was able to cast quite a few offprints of excavation reports on the table, and got the job. I still had no degree, but soon after wrote an MA thesis on the Saxon and medieval palaces at Cheddar, which made me academically respectable.

It must be stressed that up to this point I had been merely a technician. I did the digs, and I described the results. There was little or no attempt to put them into a wider framework of research, or to *explain* them. With this I was at that time content, but now I was in a different ball-game. I not only had to teach students the *synthesis* of archaeology (principally medieval, since I was in a *history* department), but was expected to do real research rather than just digging things up, to make contributions to understanding rather than mere reportage. By 1968 I was having some success in synthesizing work on the Dark Ages in Somerset, with which my digs had been especially concerned. Since 1971 (when I was 50) I have produced a steady output of papers on synthesis, and on methodology, as well as more excavation reports (for I remain active in the field). By 1978 I had published over 100 reports or books, and a quantity of more ephemeral notes and book reviews.

In that 15 years I had worked my way (or been pushed) up the academic ladder to Senior Lecturer and Reader, and was then appointed to the new Chair of Archaeology at York. In the light of my relatively non-academic background, this was a surprise (to me especially!), but also a challenge. I had by then formulated many of the ideas and attitudes expounded in this book, and I had also firm ideas on what should be learnt by archaeology and history undergraduates, and the methods by which they might most effectively learn.

The new course was set up in 1978, and the first students came in 1979, and also my first member of staff, Tania Dickinson. She was as academic as I was a 'hairy digger', and we made a good team in the early years, helped and encouraged by a series of able students, some of whom are already working in archaeology. We now have two more staff members, Harold Mytum and Steve Roskams, with degrees in archaeology and philosophy respectively.

York has been the major challenge of my life, taken on at the age of 56, which was an unusually old appointment to a Chair these days. I not only had to design a degree that would enable students to learn *how* to do things (the practical side of digging, surveying, drawing, photographing and writing); *what* the subject-matter of archaeology was – the basic *data*; and the *theory* that lay behind any attempts to use these data to increase human understanding about the past. This last was the most difficult: neither Tania nor I had been involved much in theoretical issues (as opposed to the synthesis of data), but we had to learn quickly, in order that our students should be at home in the rapidly changing field of archaeological theorizing. This had been especially dynamic in the 1970s, by the stimulation of such remarkable thinkers as Lewis Binford and David Clarke, on both sides of the Atlantic. Both our theoretical horizons have been much enlarged since 1978, and we have begun to apply what was principally theory related to *prehistoric* archaeology to our own fields in the medieval period.

I thus found myself in the curious position (rather unpredictably in the light of my background) of giving my inaugural lecture on 'The New Medieval Archaeology'. This attempted, albeit rather naively, to indicate to the university public what my subject was about, and how it had been revolutionized by the theoretical changes of the 1970s. The subtitle of my lecture was 'King Arthur and his Random Number Table', which may give some idea of its flavour, but this book is no place to expound the philosophies of the heady times we archaeologists live in.

This then, is one man's story, the only one of which I can claim any knowledge. It has illustrated one rather uncertain path to (eventually) becoming an archaeologist, and it also serves as an introduction to what archaeologists *do* all the time, the theme of my next chapter. Archaeology is not, however, just *doing*, it is also *learning*. To me, archaeology has given the education which I missed out on in my earlier life.

5

What do Archaeologists Do?

There are many different kinds of archaeologist, and each spends his time in a different way. Some broad divisions are:

(1) Those who organize archaeology: they are really managers, the people behind the scenes, who provide the administrative framework within which other archaeologists work. Such are (in England) the inspectors of ancient monuments who do in fact actually 'inspect monuments', but mainly monitor the spending of public money; and the directors of big units, like York or London, who spend much of their time in public relations work, negotiating with developers, or fund-raising. Although they are trained archaeologists of high academic calibre (like Peter Addyman at York) they rarely dig themselves, but do edit the reports their staff write.

(2) The collectors of data: these are the main archaeological work-force. They include aerial photographers, regularly flying to locate new sites shown by changes in crop growth, parch marks over buried walls, or other changes in the soil due to ancient activity which can only be appreciated from some height. There are archaeologists who walk over every field or mountain in large areas, plotting on a map all finds of pottery, flint, bone and other material, so that some idea can be gained of the density of earlier occupation or land-use at different times. Others survey every bump and hollow in the ground, and thus draw up plans of prehistoric field systems or deserted medieval villages. Many archaeologists are engaged

in watching all disturbances in the ground – by motorways, pipe-lines, or quarrying – to record any features or finds that may turn up. There are those who actually do excavation, recovering complex data from the ground or as divers below the sea. These are of course the ones best known to the public, since they are always turning up something new – 'you never know what they may find'; this work is considered more glamorous and exciting than walking over fields, but it can be just as tedious. In former times in Britain, and still in many countries, notably the Mediterranean, the basic work-force are paid workmen, recruited for that purpose; they cannot be expected to take much interest in what it all means, but can be extraordinarily perceptive about strata and practical matters, because of their wider experience in construction work or digging drains. Nowadays in Britain, the basic work-force consists of either professional low-paid diggers (often archaeology graduates) students, or volunteers. Finally, some archaeologists work indoors, collecting historical data from documents and books, to enhance the work of their colleagues in the field. Ethnographic 'collecting' will be dealt with in the next chapter.

There is obviously some overlap between all these data-collectors and our next group, the data-processors. Many people will do both in the course of their work.

(3) The processors of data: aerial photographs have to be developed and printed, and plotted onto maps, before their usefulness can be realized; surveys of earthworks, or the results of field finds plotting or monitoring destruction have to be neatly drawn up for publication. All finds recovered have to be cleaned, marked, conserved, stabilized, identified and catalogued.

The afterwork in processing data collected in an excavation is enormous, and the problem of doing so the principal reason for the frightening delays between the excavation work and its publication. So much is involved on a complex site, so many specialists are brought in, that it can take 20 years or more to get the data to publication. Even with my relatively good record of publishing my excavations, there are still several digs which I directed in the late 1950s or 1960s which are not yet published, not through any negligence on my part, but because of difficulty in getting specialist reports on bones, soil samples and so on. It is also much easier to raise funds for excavations than for post-excavation work, even though four or five times as many man-hours are required for the latter as for the former. In the Jewbury example quoted above Sainsbury's were legally bound to pay for the excavation – the 'removal of the skeletons' – but were not in any way committed to their study. Government grants given for the use of unemployed people in archaeological projects do not extend to post-excavation work. A number of archaeologists are currently employed as 'ghost-writers', preparing for publication reports of excavations which for various reasons cannot be written by the excavator – he is dead, has emigrated to Australia, has moved into a job which leaves no spare time, or is just incapable.

Specialist data-processors may work in museums or laboratories and are highly skilled, using sophisticated and expensive equipment, such as the half-million pound machine set up at Oxford to do precise radio-carbon dating from samples of organic material such as charcoal.

(4) Analysers of data: again there is no hard and fast line between (3) and (2). Many of the data-processors are also engaged in the study of objects, in an effort to impart *meaning* to them in explanatory or historical terms. Some archaeologists will collect, process, and analyse their own data, and might be hard put to say where one job began and another ended; there are nevertheless clear conceptual differences between (1) and (4), and there are many workers who will never get beyond (1), (2) or (3) to do (4) (such as technical draughtspersons). These are really technicians, who are providing the prepared basis for workers in (4) and beyond. Conversely there are those who are rarely engaged in (1)–(3) but who move in at stage (4), making 'sense' of masses of processed data.

(5) The synthesizers: synthesis may be at site level, for instance in making overall sense of hundreds of graves in a cemetery; or at a local level, considering the settlement pattern in a particular parish (see, for example Wharram

Percy in Chapter 8); or at a regional level, bringing together all data on medieval villages in a county; or at a national level, for example considering all stone circles in Britain, or every Saxon shield; or even at the international level, comparing settlements in Germany with those in France, or megaliths in Malta with those in Ireland.

Parallel to these divisions of archaeology, we are also moving up the academic ladder, from the untrained workmen to the pot-washer, from the site supervisors up to directors of excavations, up to the directors of units and the academic archaeologists in government institutions or universities. (1)–(5) are all really concerned with the *meat* of archaeology, the mass of processed and synthesized data that have accrued from many kinds of observations, and has hopefully been published.

There yet remains the really important work, (6) the *interpretation* of this material, to make meaningful statements about the past, either about *what* happened, *where* it happened, *how, when*, or more particularly in the present climate of archaeological enquiry, *why* it happened. *What* was it like to be an Iron Age smith? *Where* and *when* was iron-working first developed? *How* was it done in technical terms and, most importantly, *why* should anyone want to work iron in the first place? Why weren't people content to use stone or bronze any more? Flint tools had after all been around for thousands of years. Why was a need for change felt (if that is the explanation)? What were the economic and social factors which brought about such a revolution? And what changes resulted from such new developments in technology? Who masterminded the use of iron in any society?

By this level of archaeological work we are firmly in the academic world, in the universities or equivalent public or private institutions. Archaeologists working at this level are our 'leading lights' of the previous chapters. From such 'big' questions and possible answers come even bigger problems of pure theory: What is the relationship of rubbish to human behaviour? What general laws of human behaviour may be deduced from our understanding of the past? What is man essentially? And how does he differ from other species?

WHAT IT'S LIKE TO BE AN ARCHAEOLOGIST

In the second part of this chapter we will be more realistic; we shall move from the above abstract classification of the hierarchy of work in archaeology, and examine what it is like to be in a particular job, or to be a student. We may not know much about the daily life of a Bronze Age farmer, but we *do* know about the daily life of a student, a worker on an excavation, a full-time professional working in a major unit, and a professor of archaeology. There are many other archaeologists' daily lives which could be described, but these are the four on which I can write with some knowledge. Inevitably, these pen-portraits are only partly generalized; they are particular representatives of a class or a place; the student is, for instance, a York student; the professional is in the York Archaeological Trust, the professor of archaeology is myself.

The student

The student embarking on a degree in archaeology is usually a school-leaver. Some (and we recommend this) secure their university place and then take a year off, to travel or to get experience of 'life', and to get some digging experience, which few have acquired at school. There are also mature students who have been working in achaeology at fairly low levels for some years, who have become very interested intellectually, and who now want to know more of 'what it all means'. A few of these are welcome – their commitment makes up for their usually poor school record.

The school-leaver has usually little idea of what archaeology means. Few study it at O and A level. Surprisingly few, when they come for interview, have even read a serious book on archaeology (as opposed to *Treasures of the Past* or *Did Space-men Build Stonehenge?*) It is our job to find out, by judicious discussion, whether they do have a genuine commitment, and are likely to be suitable 'blank pages' on which we may imprint an understanding. We look for qualities of intelligence, imagination, a lively outgoing personality and a wide range of cultural interests (including science-fiction!). If we find out that they really are interested in *people* rather than *things,* we recommend them to think again, and do history, anthropology or a social science.

Having surmounted the hurdles of getting a place, the student arrives and settles in. There is a difficult first term. There are often problems about adjusting to a mode of education where one has to *learn*, not to be *taught*, and to a life of freedom and tempting vices and pleasures. The students are often homesick or suffering withdrawal symptoms on the temporary or permanent cessation of an emotional relationship. In this difficult state, everything is thrown at them – the whole apparatus of living and working on a campus, and (in the department) a welter of paper, syllabuses, reading lists, and essay topics. They are confronted by these strange people who live and breathe archaeology and who expect them to do the same. They soon find out we are actually human beings who, although we work hard, do also play hard, and do ordinary things like gardening or watching TV. With most students, we are soon on first name terms (this is a major revolution in British universities in the last decade or two).

Our students settle down to a course on York. They find out about the archaeology, architecture and history of the place where they are going to live for three years. Quite often it is the attraction of York as a famous historic city which has made them apply to us. They see York's digs, and meet the numerous archaeologists who work there in the field, in offices, and laboratories, and those who work in the archaeology of Yorkshire. There are lectures to be attended, both on York and on the principles and methods of archaeology, projects to work on, seminar papers to prepare, and essays to write. It is all rather overwhelming, but by the end of term they at least know what archaeology is really about, have made new friends, and are ready for a break in the bosom of a family Christmas (with a load of work and reading to do). In common with most university students, they develop very rapidly, so much so that their parents hardly know them; some blame us for having brought about such changes in their dear daughter or son.

In the rest of the first year they go on a residential field trip to a distant area; they learn more about the principles of collecting and analysing archaeological data, and of the practical skills of surveying and field-walking. They learn how to talk, to expound rather than read seminar papers, and study a substantial topic such as 'rural settlement and economy'. They have learnt, with varying degrees of success, how to combine work with pleasure, how to skim books without actually *reading* them, and how to cope with our incessant demands for more and better work. A group identity develops, and discussion begins to take off. The ideal seminar is one in which it wouldn't matter much if the lecturer left the room. Personal tensions have become resolved, or *modi vivendi* worked out. By the end of the year, it is clear to the students and to us who is working really hard and developing a wide understanding, and who is only doing the basic minimum to avoid getting hauled over the carpet, or in extreme cases, getting sent down. A few find in this first year that archaeology (or even university life) is not for them – they 'drop out'. The great majority do, however, cope very well with the demands of an archaeology course.

In the first summer vacation, the student does six weeks of excavation, usually on the sites that we sponsor or run. Currently these are an Iron Age and Roman inland promontory fort in west Wales, a Cistercian abbey near Birmingham, or the multi-period rural settlement site of Wharram Percy on the Yorkshire Wolds (Chapter 8). This experience provides a splendid change from indoor course work, a chance to get really fit, and a very wide social experience. Working as a team, for seven or eight hours a day, six days a week, they really get to know each other, and enjoy collecting and analysing absolutely new data. One of the things which archaeology has especially to offer is this opportunity to be right at the working-face of primary research; students frequently make important discoveries and more importantly deduce their overall significance. They soon realize that it isn't just the 'experts', the professionals, who find out all the interesting things in archaeology, it can be *them*. Most do very well in the field; there are inevitably a few Jonahs and moaners ('it's wet, it's cold, the food is awful, I've hurt my back, I've got a blister, can't we go to the pub? Yerghh, I've cut a worm in half'), and one has to admit that there are students who will do better at 'book' archaeology, and should avoid trowels, mud and wheelbarrows. This doesn't matter, archaeology needs all kinds of talent, intellectual ones especially; but it's important that all synthesizers, all *users* of archaeological data should know how they are obtained, with what blood, sweat and tears, and how reliable the published account is likely to be. (See my 'How likely is likely?', reprinted here in Chapter 7.)

The summer is formative: this is when some students really get bitten by the bug (sometimes literally!) and decide that they will become archaeologists by hook or by crook. Commitment to the subject is usually intensified, and when they return to the university in the autumn it is with an air of purpose. Further themes are studied (churches, monasteries, urbanism, burial practices) and further skills acquired (drawing, computing, photography, laboratory work). They also begin work on their own piece of research – a dissertation, in which they develop their skills at bringing data together into a form suitable for publication. Some are of a remarkably high standard, and some do eventually get published, an invaluable step in a professional career.

Assessment looms large in student minds; although entrenched in university structure in Britain, and in the expectations of contemporary society, it is not what education should be about. But we have to grade and to rank, and the competitive element does, in our socially undeveloped society, act as a spur to hard work. An eye to the material rewards of 'doing well' is a powerful incentive, however distasteful this may seem to those of us who see universities as places to foster intellectual development. Assessment is by a number of examiners, including one from another university, and is based on a broad spectrum of effort: dissertation, lecture, seminar, portfolio, field-work, and written examinations. When all this is finished, there is the grand ceremony of degree day, when we all wear our academic finery, and proud parents see their offspring hooded and gowned, receiving BA degrees at the hands of the Chancellor.

Graduates who are outstanding may go on to do research for a higher degree, but these are increasingly rare, not because of shortage of talent but because (in the 1980s) of financial restrictions imposed by an economically-orientated central government in Britain.

The rest try to get jobs, short or long-term. Any experience here is valuable, however lowly it may seem at the time. The important thing is to survive, and preferably by doing archaeology. Some decide to opt out and seek more lucrative offers in the civil service, merchant banking or industrial management.

One skill that is being learnt is how to work in archaeology while surviving by social security. Increasing unemployment may well make this more acceptable in our society; and monetary benefits may be more readily available in future to those who are working at something worthwhile.

We hope that even if our students don't become full-time 'professionals' or 'gainfully unemployed', archaeology will remain an important part of their lives, to be worked at as and when opportunity offers, notably in early retirement.

The worker on an excavation

What happens on an excavation needs a book to itself, and the reader is referred to the long sections on excavation in all the standard textbooks. Here we can do no more than delineate what one would see if one visited an excavation and saw people at work. I describe here the scene at Wharram Percy, which should be read in association with the wider aspects of that site, dealt with as a case-study in Chapter 8.

On a big excavation like this, where over 100 people are sometimes involved, there is a considerable infrastructure. The work is done mainly on a rota system, with only one professional (the cook). So we see people preparing vegetables, washing-up, and emptying latrines. Some faithful volunteers maintain the hot showers, repair tools and survey equipment, make benches, and cut up wood for the fire. In the case of Wharram, Professor Maurice Beresford (a medieval economic historian) master-minds these activities; without such management skills, the whole archaeological edifice would crumble. If we eavesdropped on his morning briefing after breakfast, we'd hear the jobs being assigned and the shortcomings of those who left the gates open, or left their late night 'coffocoa' mug unwashed. There would be a weather forecast (wet, cold and windy), a report on the state of a 'lurgi' affecting diggers (a bug that lives at Wharram and comes out each year to give people stomach upsets – in Spain it's there all the time!), and any interesting news, such as war breaking out in a far-away real world, or important visitors expected; lectures, walks, excursions and films being organized.

By 9.15 am everyone is at work. The major activity to be seen now is digging. The workers are also finding things, such as bones, pot, stone tools or charcoal. These are being put into bags or containers marked to indicate precisely where they were found. Plastic labels in waterproof ink are being written to affix to the ground. Every different area of soil, every hole, every wall, every patch of stones, in fact every *context* has its own number and description; these may run into hundreds or thousands on the average excavation.

The site supervisor sees to all this; he supervises other less experienced workers and also digs himself. Periodically he will straighten up and stretch (trowelling induces muscle cramp) and make notes; these are on special proforma *context* sheets which have spaces for every possible kind of observation: what a layer is like, how far it extends, what it seals, what was above it, how it relates to other contexts, and what it 'means'. There are spaces for sketches and photographs, and notes on finds. The compilation of these context sheets is the basic *record*, together with drawings on which all else depends. The skilful filling in of a context sheet, together with later editing, is a very difficult job, and demands much thought and concentration. There must not be too much noise (no idle chatter or transistor radios, please); all that should be heard is the gentle clink of a trowel on stones, the swush-swush of brushes, measurements being called out, an earnest discussion on interpretation, the munching of cows, and the high noise of larks.

Other workers are using survey instruments, drawing

patterns of stones, sections of soil, and measuring the position of finds. Periodically, photographs are taken. The finds and drawings are taken to nearby huts, tents or caravans. Drawings are inked in and neat copies made, context sheets are being checked, and the finds go to a special finds department, run by a finds supervisor, who will organize their cleaning and marking. The finds are then 'viewed' by site supervisor and director, to assess their date and significance, classified, catalogued, and bagged or boxed. There may well be specialists at this stage – on our site we have a caravan specially set up for classifying and drawing pottery (the latter after the bits have been stuck together), and for identifying animal bones.

An important figure is the photographer. He goes round all parts of the site at regular intervals in a Land Rover loaded with cameras. Photographs are taken in monochrome and colour, slides and prints, using a high tripod, the Land Rover roof, or a high photographic tower. He keeps a record of each take, and these are recorded in his index, and noted in the excavation records. Later he will supply contact prints to the supervisors.

The director of the excavation has done a lot before the excavation starts, deciding where and how to dig, organizing the transport of the equipment to the site, laying out the space around the dig, organizing money, stationery and consumables, and generally seeing that all systems are 'go' by the time most of the work-force arrives. His job is then to see that all goes well, to encourage people, to deliver rockets if something has gone wrong, to check recording, discuss interpretation, assess finds, and generally try to keep track of everything that is happening. He may keep his own notebook on any general points of interpretation, or walk round the site periodically, talking into a tape recorder. I have also recently begun to talk to a video camera while filming what I'm talking about. The director also has to keep up morale and quell mutinies, usually in appalling weather. He usually does this by sending round a bottle of whisky for communal swigging (an object often found in the backfill of archaeologists' trenches); or stops the whole job, piles everyone into the Land

Rover and takes them to the nearest pub, or if too hot, to the Wharram Lake.

The director also digs, either (as in my case) because he likes shifting dirt from one place to another, or to be closely involved in crucial areas where he needs to *see* exactly what relationships are being revealed, and to make sure their significance is fully appreciated and recorded. When he does 'move in' on an area in this way, the site supervisor's morale drops!

The workers, and especially the supervisors, should be kept in touch with all that is being done and discussed, new data that have been found, or new theories propounded. This is absolutely crucial if everyone is to work meaningfully, and is usually done after tea. An uninformed digger is a bad and unhappy one.

The responsibility for writing up the site for publication rests on the director; the better he is at making sure that all records are properly kept, the easier this will be (as we have learnt by bitter experience). Workers rarely learn how to record properly *until* they have had to write up an excavation (which is difficult to arrange!). Increasingly we try to involve many people in post-excavation to underline the necessity of good recording.

Finally the dig is finished, and all data have been extracted from the ground. This is when most of the work-force remember pressing engagements elsewhere, leaving a few heroic figures (including the director) to the back-breaking task of dismantling, cleaning and transporting the equipment, vehicles and stores. The director can usually rely on some faithful helpers to stay on (usually arranged beforehand) for a day or two, to pack everything away.

So much for the excavation itself. There are often other things going on, which although not digging, or providing the infrastructure, are part of the project as a whole. We may see people making a record of plants and flowers now growing in the environment (were they always there?), catching small mammals in boxes at night: they like this, it's warm, and the same ones come back the next night. Others will be recording the gravestones or measuring the church and drawing it stone by stone; 'laying out' excavated buildings for visitor displays; showing visitors around (a good exercise for the diggers), and finally going round local fields and farms, recording finds in the ploughsoil, assessing modes of current land-exploitation and management, and recording old people's memories of former times.

This account of what its like to work on an excavation probably gives a rosy view, based as it is on a research dig taking place in an isolated rural landscape. This is very different from working in a town, as my next section shows.

The professional in a unit

The world of the big urban unit, like the York Archaeological Trust, is altogether more professional than most other excavations. This is not to say that the archaeology is better, or the staff more committed, but there is obviously a very different atmosphere on digs that go on for several months compared with those that last only a few weeks. It is difficult to keep up enthusiasm in these circumstances, especially when the digging goes on throughout the winter in very unpleasant conditions of mud and cold. Only the toughest professionals can take this sort of thing and at the same time keep up efficient recording. A very tight team spirit develops in these circumstances and a certain *machismo*.

The urban unit exists to deal with the archaeology of an important historic town, notably with the threats that arise from development and renewal. At York there has to be close collaboration with the City Council, the planning authority, to find out what development is approved in this year, next year, or sometime in the near future. Once the scale and nature of development is known, the firm or contractor is contacted and informed of the archaeological potential of the area to be destroyed. Very often the developers are interested, for the sake of their public image, if nothing else, and give extensive support in cash or in kind, as Lloyds Bank and the General Accident Insurance Company have done in York.

City digs are complex. In York there are nineteen centuries of archaeology, and deposits can be seven or eight metres deep. They are immensely rich in structures and finds, and

74

the conditions of preservation allow a great deal of organic evidence to survive: structures and objects of wood, leather, textile; mosses, beetles, plants and seeds; micro-organisms such as stomach parasites (York's cesspits provide a rich haul for the environmental scientist), and metal objects in pristine condition. Occasionally the finds are extremely valuable as well as historically important; a 1982 example was the discovery in a pit in York of a helmet of the eighth century, now insured for half a million pounds.

Not all threats can be coped with. There have to be discussions on priorities: what must be dealt with by a big and expensive excavation, what need only be trenched, and what can be largely written off with no more than observance of the destruction. A dig in the first category was Coppergate, which explored some of the richest Viking levels in Europe.

The staff of the Trust number nearly a hundred. There are usually several excavation teams active at any one time, each with its supervisor and site finds department. At the Trust's headquarters there are draftspersons, conservators, pottery specialists, photographers, and finds researchers. At the University there is an entire Environmental Archaeology Unit, with several full-time staff paid for by central government resources, who work on all the non-archaeological 'finds' that come from York's rich waterlogged soils. It is estimated that a cubic metre of Coppergate's deposits contains half a million 'items' of scientific interest, many of which can be seen only under a powerful microscope.

There are people writing reports for publication in York's special series, and others editing them. There is of course an office staff to keep all this going – typing the reports, feeding data into a computer, paying salaries and maintaining co-ordination throughout the organization.

All this is the archaeology of York as planned research. There is also, however, in this case a quite separate organization, Cultural Resource Management Limited, whose staff handle all publicity, fund-raising, and the making and selling of souvenirs, replicas, Eric Blood-Axe mugs and T-shirts, postcards and slides. There is a special shop in York where such things are sold, and a mail-order branch. CRM makes profits of many thousands of pounds which help to keep the archaeological research going. This is likely to be increasingly important in the future, as central government gives less and less money, and looks with more favour on such schemes of 'privatization'.

At the head of this efficient organization is the Director, Peter Addyman, a former university lecturer who chose to be at the sharp and professional end of archaeology rather than the sheltered life of academia and students. He and his senior staff keep tight control over all the diverse activities of the Trust; they see that the publications come out regularly and are of high quality; they also disseminate the results to the archaeological world by lecturing to conferences and universities in Britain and abroad, notably in Scandinavia and the USA. Peter keeps himself cognizant with all that goes on, but has to spend much of his time on non-research activities, sitting on committees, giving lecture tours, securing royal and noble patronage. Queen Margarethe of Denmark is an invaluable patron, and takes an informed academic interest in the work. Prince Charles, who read archaeology at Cambridge, has also been very active in securing support.

The Trust takes its educational role very seriously. Its most ambitious venture is a major new museum, built on the Coppergate site, the Jorvik Viking Centre. This is no ordinary museum of objects in glass cases and explanatory labels. After paying admission, the visitor (and half a million a year are expected) sits in a small electric 'time-capsule' car. He is then taken on a time-travel tour backwards through the last ten centuries emerging into a reconstruction of Viking Coppergate. He moves slowly through a Viking Street, where there are houses, rubbish, cats, excrement, people quarrelling, trading and making things. All the appropriate noises are flung at the visitor in 64-speaker ambient sound; the sound of people nattering and chattering in a market was recorded by Icelanders in Reykjavik. There are smells of fish, cooking, tanning, wood-smoke and dung assailing the nostrils. The time-cars approach the river where a Viking ship is moored, unloading its goods.

The cars then turn a corner and enter a replica of the

archaeological excavation, where the time-traveller returns to 1980, and sees the evidence for all that he has experienced with all his senses in the first part of the trip. Finally he comes out into a splendid 'Artefact Hall', a spectacular display of finds, and a shop where he can buy books, souvenirs, and replicas.

This imaginative and educational project is a worthy climax to ten years of digging in York, and will do a great deal to interest the general public in what archaeology really means, in a way that can be fully understood by everybody.

The professor of archaeology

Professors write books, among other things; and that is what I am doing now, on Christmas Day. I am sitting on a balcony of a room in a hotel in southern Spain, basking in hot sunshine, and occasionally leaving my writing to go down for a swim in the sea across the road, or more warmly in the heated swimming pool below my balcony. In the afternoon my wife and I will walk into the hills behind the hotel to do some ethnoarchaeology, a subject which will figure in my next chapter.

This is all very pleasant, but what else do professors of archaeology do?

My life is spent roughly equally between administration, teaching and research. The administration is necessary because every professor has a role in running the university, sitting on committees, being part of the governing hierarchy under the leadership of the Vice-Chancellor. Most of my administrative duties lie, however, in running my department. This is not an autonomous organization, it is part of the university, with very close links with the central administration. They handle all the admissions, fees, and accommodation of archaeology students; and provide the entire financial framework within which we operate. We are a relatively small and inexpensive department, in comparison with the 'giants' of physics, chemistry, biology or English; we are responsible for the expenditure of hardly more than a quarter of a million pounds a year.

My experience in York was perhaps rather different from that of other professors (apart from the obvious superiority of York to other universities!). I did, after all, as described above, have to design new degrees in detail, before I had other staff to advise me; so my first year at York was entirely devoted to getting degrees off the ground, before my first staff and students arrived.

Much time is taken up with answering letters. These vary enormously; there are requests for information on courses, enquiries about excavations past and current, letters from cranks who have found a Roman villa or a stone circle in their garden, or have worked out King Arthur's pedigree. There are invitations to give lectures to conferences, local archaeological societies, seminars to other departments of archaeology; to write a book for Basil Blackwell, or take part in a TV programme. There are requests for references for past students, and letters from them seeking advice. There are funds to be accounted for, problems about insurance, fire precautions, building maintenance (we are in an eighteenth century house, a historic monument itself), and heating. My efficient and percipient secretary sorts all these through for me, and very often compiles suitable answers which are far better than anything I could write; these I then read and sign.

Teaching takes up a lot of my time. In a small department, the professor has to pull his weight, as well as making his own influence felt on students. In an average week in term time, I may spend ten hours in direct teaching – lecturing and tutoring – and many more in preparing lectures, chairing seminars, setting and marking essays, sorting out students' academic and personal problems, and just talking to them about their work or life in general. The more a professor is seen by his students, the more effective he is as head of department. In the winter he interviews prospective students, and in the summer he faces the lengthy process of setting and marking examinations, having examiners' meetings, deciding on and awarding degrees.

Apart from teaching to both archaeology and history undergraduates, there is the more demanding postgraduate teaching and supervision. Finally in the summer vacation, a full eight weeks is totally taken up with excavations, their preparation and dealing with their aftermath, and the number of student contact hours here is probably more than the whole of the rest of the year put together. But this is also part of my research, so much of this time belongs under the heading of my final responsibility of doing research.

University lecturers are, strange though it may seem, not appointed because they can administer or teach; no evidence of being able to do either of these things is asked for when one applies for a job. Nor is any formal training given to those who have no experience whatever of either (though this is changing). The sole criterion is research, whether the candidate is a scholar of some reputation in his own field, as witnessed especially by his list of publications, and by his referee's remarks. It is on the corporate research of its staff that the university bases its reputation. On appointment, one is expected to continue to publish and keep in the forefront of one's subject. Students obviously benefit from all this; teaching in a university may not be as efficient as it might be, but should be at the highest possible level in terms of giving a student a scholarly and up-to-date view of work in a particular topic.

Once appointed, the professor is expected not only to continue to be a leading light in his field, but also to lead his staff. Normally they will already have special areas of interest, but the professor should be able to encourage and advise them, and try to organize the work of the department so that they can pursue research effectively, and incorporate it in the teaching. In this way the students feel they are part of a research institution and will be proud to belong to it.

My own research is done principally in the evenings, weekends, and vacations, as in term time, administration and teaching take up most of the time. But, as I tell my students, there *are* 168 hours in a week, and one has to learn to make the most of them and of the vacations.

A lot of my research time is spent in writing up to the stage of publication the results of excavations that I have directed. This involves basic ordering of the data, and putting the results into a wider structure of knowledge. For instance, I am currently engaged in writing up work on an Anglo-Saxon church at Deerhurst, a Bronze Age barrow in Yorkshire, and our long-term work at Wharram Percy (Chapter 8).

Some more general research may arise from these reports. For instance, as a result of writing up a big Dark Age cemetery in Somerset, I got interested in why people orientate graves to different points of the compass. I gathered together all the data I could on the subject, and a publication called 'Grave orientation' was the result. This treated the subject not within the narrow confines of Dark Age Somerset, but in different parts of the world through time. When I excavated an Anglo-Saxon watermill at Tamworth, I knew nothing about such things, but I soon found out, and have since taken this on as a major research topic.

Much time is also spent on reading books on archaeology, keeping abreast of at least the areas we teach, though even this is increasingly difficult with the enormous amount now being written. My own research is not typical of most professors of archaeology in that I don't write major works of synthesis of other people's published work (only reviews of them) and so am not so dependent on library facilities as many of my fellow professors. Most of my work derives from the field, not from books. An increasingly important part of my time is spent not only in excavating, but in travel, a form of open-air research especially appropriate for archaeologists, and involving far less organization than excavation. This form of travel with a research purpose is called ethnoarchaeology, and is the subject of my next chapter.

The life of a professor of archaeology is then a full one, full of hard work, challenge and stimulation, and on the whole a very satisfying final stage in my career.

When, the reader may ask, do I *live*? Well, to me, archaeology *is* life, and other things (and people) tend to get ruthlessly pushed aside for it. Fortunely my children are now all grown-up with their own families, and my wife (she also works in archaeology as a freelancer) and I are free to do a good deal with our 168-hour weeks. We *do* do other things; when I get tired, I *stop,* and watch Dallas or Mash. We read novels at bedtime and do a lot of exercise to keep fit, and we listen to music continuously when we are working. Unlike many people I cannot work in silence – I need a wall of music to shut me in with my thoughts or my drawing. So, on the whole it's a good life: digging, travelling, drawing, writing, and *talking*.

TOOLS AND TECHNIQUES: EXCAVATION AND ANALYSIS

Archaeological excavation is a complex team operation. How it is done will depend on the aims of the work, the resources available (of people, money and time), the kind of subsoil, and the type of site. In large-scale rescue digging, large machines may be used to strip off the upper layers. At Dorestad, in Holland, most of a town of the eighth–ninth centuries was stripped, covering many hectares; units of excavation here were 40×20 m (800 square metres) and each took only a few days with 20–30 workers. At the other extreme, the excavation of a single grave with many finds may take one person a week or more. At Wharram Percy (Chapter 8) a careful hand-excavation of 400 square metres took us five seasons of three weeks with an average of a dozen workers.

Apart from powered machines, the ordinary tools of spade, fork, hoe, pick and shovel are in common use for the heavy work, where a lot of soil has to be shifted. If a ten foot deep ditch is to be emptied of the dirt which has filled it over the centuries, careful use of smaller tools would make little impression. The standard tool for more careful work is, however, the small mason's pointing trowel with a diamond-shaped blade; on a dig everyone will have his or her own trowel in hand or in back pocket. In dry conditions this is used with a hand brush, with a hand shovel and small bucket to carry away the dirt to a wheelbarrow, dumper truck, or onto a heap.

The area to be dug may be as small as one metre square (test-holes to sample a large area), or trenches one or two metres wide (for instance to cut a section through a Roman road). Most modern excavation is, however, done in areas ranging from 10×10 m units upwards. Depths can range from no more than 20–30 cms in open rural areas to the 6-8 m encountered in deep urban deposits such as those of York or London, where town-dwelling has caused the accumulation of millions of tonnes of dirt and building debris.

The principle of excavation is to peel off accumulated layers of dirt one at a time, beginning with the turf and topsoil, until all humanly-derived material has been removed, and natural undisturbed subsoil or rock is exposed over the site. On the way down, many features will be encountered, such as ditches, post-holes, wall foundations, pits and graves. These are found by noting differences in soil colour or composition, shapes or patterns which indicate to the experienced eye where there has been an ancient structure or disturbance. To see these things, the work has to be done very cleanly, with no loose dirt or mess, and with clean straight edges. Each layer or feature has to be separately defined, numbered and removed, a careful record being made in drawings, photo-graphs and words of its appearance, composition and extent. The position of any finds – pottery, metal, glass, stone, etc. – is also recorded.

Excavation is destruction; normally at the end of the dig nothing remains except the natural rock, clay or gravel, with the shapes of holes cut in it by the features, such as ditches, whose fills have been removed. The only exceptions are where walls or floors are encountered which will be preserved for people to see. Many visitors to digs are disappointed to find that what they are looking at and having explained to them will be removed or filled in again. The sad fact is that if anything like a wall or a floor, or even the post-holes of a palace hall are left open, they will very quickly deteriorate from weather, animals or vandalism unless a lot of money is spent in conservation and aftercare.

The dig finished, the site is filled in by machine or by hand, and the work of analysing the results begins. Many digs never get published at all, and the work in the field is seen as unjustified destruction of the evidence without record. Excavators lose heart, move on to jobs which leave them no time, emigrate or die; or are just incapable of bringing the work to publication. In all these cases, it would have been better if the dig had never been done at all.

The post-excavation work is indeed complex, and demands skills which are more rare than those needed in excavation. Finds have to be conserved, drawn and reported on by specialists. A report on a big cemetery such as Jewbury for example, will involve human biologists for months or years examining and measuring the human skeletons, to find out about public health, life expectancy, diseases, and the make-up of the buried population. The written or computerized records and especially the drawings have to be collated, analysed, and made sense of. Whereas in the excavation work proceeds from the latest levels to the most ancient, say from modern through medieval to the lowest Roman levels, in post-excavation analysis the process is reversed. The sequence of occupation is reconstructed in phases, beginning with earliest and ending with the modern.

Text, drawings, and photographs are finally assembled for publication and go through the usual process of computerized or other typesetting, proofs and binding. Increasingly a large part of the work is computerized, by the use of word-processors and automated typesetting, and there is a tendency for much of the detail to go not into hard print, but into a microfiche. This is a sheet of film with miniaturized trans-parencies which can be examined by the use of a special reader or powerful magnifying glass; on a single sheet of film there can be 96 pages of text or drawing. A copy of this is inserted into a pocket in the back of every copy of the publication, and can reduce the cost considerably.

Modern archaeological reports, unlike (I hope) this book are difficult for the non-archaeologist to understand, increasingly technical, scientific, and complex. Yet they are the basic record of what was found (and destroyed), and form the basis of all current and future research. Just as the modern dig recovers more evidence than those of 20, 50, or 100 years ago, so the amount of detail published increases in propor-tion. In 1979, a trial excavation was done on two Roman villas at Wharram Percy. A total of 50 square metres was dug in small holes or trenches. About 15 people worked in the field on this for four days. The resultant report, which we are just about to publish, has taken five years to get together, and will be a monograph of about 100 pages with 37 figures, with a further 100+ pages in microfiche.

It is a pleasant moment for the director of an excavation when the printed copies of the report arrive, to be distributed to friends and colleagues. This is the end-product of a long process which began with the pregnant decision 'let's have an excavation here.'

6

Ethnoarchaeology, or How to Avoid Boring Holidays

Ever since 'civilized' man moved out of his environment, and explored distant areas of the world where white men were an unfamiliar sight, he has evinced great interest in encountering peoples and societies whose life-style, economy and beliefs were fundamentally different from those of Europe. Such peoples appeared to be 'primitive' and 'backward', ignorant of such basic things as the necessity to be decently dressed, the using of money, smelting metals, or knowing about wheels and machines. Since European man of the sixteenth century and later believed himself to be a very admirable creature, it was only a short step to regarding people of less sophisticated culture as 'inferior', suitable for extermination or exploitation in the interests of European prosperity.

A further more interesting stage was to think that perhaps in these peoples we could see a living representation of what our society had been like in prehistoric times. Hunter–gatherers in Africa, Australia or the New World provided analogues for our own pre-farming life. Flint, stone and bone tools found in prehistoric European contexts were compard with those still in use in remote areas, and their function thereby 'explained'. If, for example, a particular form of bone tool found in prehistoric Europe, whose function could not be guessed at, was exactly like one still used by Eskimos for skinning a seal, then it was assumed that was what our ancient tool was also used for. This was perhaps rather a naive way of reasoning, but it did begin the vast subject of cross-cultural correlation, in all parts of the world, and at all times, which has been such an important element in the development of modern world archaeology.

In the nineteenth and twentieth centuries, remote peoples at different cultural and technical levels have been a happy hunting ground for anthropologists. The latter increasingly became interested, not so much in seeking analogies for tools, but in the whole systems by which those people lived: their marriage, property and inheritance customs; ranking in society, religious beliefs, and art; stages of life from infancy through puberty, adolescence, maturity and old age. These have become the classic agenda of social anthropology, the field study being known as ethnography (physical anthropology is concerned with racial types and human biology).

For a long time anthropologists studying remote peoples as ethnographers did so from a superior stance, rather as if the people being studied were some kind of super-monkey. Hand-in-hand with missionaries, soldiers and traders, they were the agents of oppression and had little real respect for other peoples' cultures, or for the idea that there might be alternative ways of living, rather than inferior ones. On the other hand, the idea of the 'noble savage', the purer and less corrupt life of the primitive, also influenced even nineteenth-century anthropologists.

ETHNOGRAPHY TODAY

Things have changed. With the decline in a general belief in the ethics of colonialism and an increasing scepticism about the quality of life in the modern industrialized world (or even its chances of survival), there is a much greater respect (and even in some cases a sort of 'Garden of Eden' envy) for the life-styles of Kalahari Bushmen, Alaskan Eskimos, or Australian aborigines. The latter are regarded nowadays as one of the most successful races in achieving a stable balance with the environment for 40,000 years. Ethnographers now approach their 'subjects' with something like humility, even though the last thing these remote peoples want to do is stay 'primitive' – they too want radios, TVs, motorcars and towns. In Ghana in 1966 I paid labourers 7s. 6d. a day (37.5 modern English pence) to work on my excavation. They did not need the money for the necessities of life, for those were provided by their community. What they saved up their wages for were transistor radios and football boots.

Although social anthropology has, through ethnography, built up a colossal world data-base for its subject, it has in recent decades been little interested in material culture or, rather surprisingly, in the *origins* of things and in their dynamics through time. Ethnographers are interested in living peoples, what they are doing *right now*. There is astonishingly little common ground with archaeology, even at Cambridge, where students study both subjects as part of the same degree.

WHAT IS ETHNOARCHAEOLOGY?

Archaeologists interested in the material culture of other societies have had to do their own ethnography, and called it ethnoarchaeology. It was not for instance until 1972 that the technical and economic base of aboriginal society was studied by archaeologists, and by then it was almost too late.

Ethnoarchaeology is the study of the *material culture* of *living* societies, which now include not only hunter–gatherers or farmers living in Africa, South America, the Arctic, Australia or the Far East, but also societies nearer to our own such as more remote areas of Europe, and even our own society. This is the *archaeology of ourselves* or, as it is now fashionably called, Modern Material Culture – MMC.

While modern ethnoarchaeologists are still interested in examining the life of hunter–gatherers and asking the simple question, 'could hunter–gatherers in Europe in 20,000 BC have been living in similar ways?' their motivation is rather more complex. The reasons for doing ethnoarchaeology may be summed up as follows:

(1) To *record* material culture – tools, building types,

technical devices, clothing, food processing equipment, beds, boats, mills, argricultural practices – which are fast disappearing under the onslaught of industrialization and mass communication. This is intrinsically interesting on its own account, and will be much more so for posterity, whatever use we or they may make of these data. Currently most of such recording is by writing, photographing, and drawing, with some use of a tape-recorder or cine camera. In future, however, with the advent of the portable video camera, the record can be much more comprehensive.

(2) To study the relationship between material culture and human behaviour, since in living societies we can ascertain what human beings are doing (or appear to be doing), and very often why they are doing it (if we can believe them!). We can see what is the by-product – the rubbish – which arises out of human behaviour. We can consider how its patterns (for example, the way rubbish is distributed around a house) are the result of what is happening in the society. Patterns of artefacts may, we learn, be wholly functional (for example, being kept away from sleeping areas) or be derived from more subtle cosmological beliefs. For instance, in one African society, the very plan of the family house is anthropomorphic – one end is regarded as the 'head' (where males work), the other is the 'excretory' end (where the females work). All rubbish must be kept at this end and not round the head, as in the living body. While not flattering to females, this is the explanation for the distribution of rubbish which an archaeologist might later find.

(3) To test traditional inferences about such relationships which may have been generated in archaeological theory, and to build up a body of new archaeological theory which will help in the interpretation of the remains of long extinct peoples. Note the difference between this approach and the older one of saying 'here in this cave we have the debris of hunter–gatherers of the end of the last Ice Age. The debris bears striking resemblance to this African hunter–gatherer group that we are now studying; therefore our prehistoric group lived like they do.'

An example of this is the classic case of Millie's Camp

(Bonnichsen, 1973). This was a trappers' camp in the Canadian Rockies used by indigenous Indians. Archaeologists came across it a few weeks after it had been abandoned. There were the remains of shelters, hearths, traps, appliances, tree carvings, clothing, waste material, food and drink wrappers, cosmetics, toys, tobacco tins, and some odd patterns of things which looked very 'ritual'. The 177 'finds' included a label from 'Rider Cowboy' jeans, plastic hair curlers, a Dinky toy Land Rover, a yellow toy parachute jumper, the arms of a white plastic toy skeleton, a Kodak film wrapper, bags from 'Robin Hood Quick Oats' and 'Aunt Jemima' pancake mix, and pages from 'Eaton's Catalogue'. The archaeologists made a detailed plan and catalogue, and, using established archaeological principles of inference, wrote a report on such matters as local resources, 'activity areas', the size of the family and its composition, how many people, what sex, their economy, their technology, religion, life-style, and how long they had been there. They then talked to Millie, who had been one of the camp's inhabitants. She was surprised, co-operative, amused, and articulate when she learnt that the archaeologists wanted to know the whole 'truth' about the camp. She accompanied them back to the site, and gave them a complete run-down on exactly who was who, what was what, and what had been going on there. The archaeologists were, of course, wrong in almost every respect. But they were now able to make a formal comparison between their own 'model' of life at Millie's camp and as it really was, and see where and how their basic inferences were wrong. Next time they interpreted the remains found on an archaeological site of prehistoric Canadian trapper–hunters, they were presumably more cautious, sadder, and wiser men.

Their experience is directly related to our final category:

(4) The expanding of mental horizons. People used to travel to widen their cultural horizons. A lot of people now travel, see nothing, attempt to understand nothing, and come back as ignorant as they went. When an archaeologist travels, he sees and observes, and his whole store of knowledge and understanding increases. In looking at the material culture of other countries we can, *as students,* not necessarily as

researchers, learn an enormous amount which we could not learn by staying at home (except by watching TV programmes about distant places). We can learn about many different ways of doing things – ploughing with oxen or camels, building wooden houses, making objects in wood or metal, ways of preparing and cooking food, how primitive machinery works, how land is irrigated, how fish are caught, how boats are made, how a windmill works, how butter and cheese are made, how the entire economy of an island works, and how people interact with the forces of nature.

ETHNOARCHAEOLOGY AROUND THE MEDITERRANEAN

I have chosen these examples deliberately – they are not what one would learn by living with New Guinea farmers, or trekking with aborigines. They are things that can be seen in Europe, notably in Greece, Turkey, Yugoslavia, Spain, and (just across the Straits) in Morocco. These are poor countries where modern things like tractors and refrigerators are beyond many people's means. They are places where the material culture is archaic, the technology and economy primitive by Western European standards.

The things we see are more akin to what medieval Britain must have been like in many ways. Thus the medieval archaeologist like myself, or any archaeologist who seeks a wider understanding of how things work, can widen his own cultural experience of such things enormously. Life in present-day Britain or America gives us little insight into what things were like in the past. We can read books, we can talk to very old people, but we can also travel and see these things *being done*.

Whilst it would still be simplistic to say 'here is village life in a high mountain area of northern Spain, there is no electricity, no mains water, no gas, no cars, everything is done by hand', therefore, 'this is what life must have been like in a Yorkshire village in the fourteenth century', one has, however, much more insight into what life could have been like, *at that level of technology*; and it must be said that the pictures of peasant life depicted in loving detail in the fourteenth century Luttrell Psalter are remarkably like scenes one can witness in Turkey or Morocco (given different climates, clothing, and people's faces).

What I am stressing is that ethnoarchaeology at this *educational*, relatively simple level is not an abstruse academic topic, as my categories (2) and (3) above are. Anyone can observe and learn in category (4), and with a little experience anyone can join in category (1) of ethnoarchaeology and *record*.

ETHNOARCHAEOLOGY ON THE CHEAP

To do such work in Europe it is not necessary to have major research funds or elaborately equipped expeditions. It is cheap, and within everybody's reach. It can make a holiday a stimulating and educational experience, rather than just lying in the sun, drinking, or finding the nearest discothéque (the three main attractions figured in holiday brochures).

In the last part of this chapter, I will describe some of the ethnoarchaeology that my wife and I have done in the last ten years, and how it is related to any of my four categories of motivation or justification outlined above. The reader may not be convinced that our experience has been very academic, but its basic enjoyment will I hope be clear.

Even the package holiday-makers see something of the different cultures of high sun/low rainfall areas. Excursions take them to local markets, but their preoccupation is principally with picking up some cheap bargain of leather or textile. If they notice the 'natives', it is not with respect or even curiosity, and they certainly wouldn't like them to marry their sons and daughters. Yet much can be seen in ordinary holiday areas, often within 5 or 10 kilometres of the Costa Brava, the Costa del Sol, or further afield, in the coastal resorts of Turkey, the Greek Islands, or anywhere along the North African coast. Much of what is to be seen and observed is of course directly relevant to our understanding of the antiquity of classical times, Byzantium, or Islam, but is also

very educational in more general ways to an archaeologist of
Northern Europe.

My examples are classified in seven main headings, all related
to the reasons for doing ethnoarchaeology outlined above.
These are: (a) appreciation of basic land forms, geology,
topography, climate: environmental archaeology; (b) understanding of the economy of areas or whole countries, often
unchanged for hundreds of years, if now rapidly being
abandoned north of the Mediterranean, and how that economy is interwoven with social life and custom; (c) the archaeology of subsistence, arable and pastoral farming, marine
resources, and the vast areas still given over to those staples of
classical times, the grape and the olive; (d) technology,
archaic kinds of machinery, sometimes also going back to the
first millennium AD: the threshing 'machine', wheeled or
pack transport, and (of especial interest to us) the watermill;
(e) daily life in remote communities: homes, food preparation
and cooking; (f) mortuary behaviour: the archaeology of
death and burial; (g) religion and value systems.

The environment

It's important for an archaeologist to understand the environment, and man's interaction with it. One can observe the
land-forms, geology, water and climate, and note the ways in
which these determine the resources available in an area at any
time, the subsistence strategies, and what types of surplus are
likely to be available for exchanging for things which cannot
be locally produced. Archaeologists of the post-classical
period have noted massive deposits of soil and stones which
fill valleys and estuaries, dated to the seventh–eighth centuries
AD (Vita-Finzi, 1969). This 'younger fill' as it is called, has
been attributed to the breakdown of the classical civilization.
There was no longer a market for agricultural produce, the

field revetments were neglected, and heavy winter rains washed out the soil that had been so carefully accumulated for centuries before.

The same kind of thing can be seen happening today, but for very different reasons. Many of the old terraced fields of the Mediterranean coastal areas are being abandoned to grass or scrub, as their owners gradually sell out to speculative builders; the old farms are falling into ruin, the field edges being broken down, and the soil washing out in the winter rains and the flood-water from the melting snows of the sierras.

The economy

Away from the coasts of the Mediterranean, much of the older exchange systems are still operating. Country produce – vegetables, fruit, wine – floods into towns like Madrid or Rome, in what is today a money economy. Country towns act as nuclei for rural areas around them, providing markets, judiciary and banking systems and other 'central place' facilities. This is not so strange, as much of this kind of system operates in Britain. In North Africa, however, earlier systems of more direct exchange are still operating, which are more like those of medieval Europe.

In Morocco, there are a few large cities which act only partly as control places; they all have different functions in the country as a whole. Tangier is the gateway to the Mediterranean, a cosmopolitan port. Casablanca is the principal port for the importation of industrial products from northern Europe: this is where you (or a wholesaler) go to buy a car, a washing machine, or a television. Rabat is the centre of government, where the king lives, where the National Museum is to be found (and very interesting it is), where the army has its headquarters. Fez is the centre of culture and learning, with its arts and crafts specialists; its university is one of the oldest in Europe, several centuries older than Oxford or Cambridge. Finally Marrakesh is a great rural centre for the Berber areas of the Atlas mountains.

Marrakesh, a good deal further south than the other

'functional' cities, is the only one of these that has as its primary role that of a great nucleus of exchange and social concourse. In the early hours of the morning lorries converge on the city bringing in goods from a wide radius. By late morning, many thousands of people are thronging the markets and enjoying themselves in the enormous 'square'. This has been called a 'permanent 7-ring circus'. Here every day, there are groups of musicians, dancers, performing animals, reciters from the Koran, magicians and conjurers, blind beggars, water-sellers, purveyors of aphrodisiacs and strange herbs and remedies, drug-peddlers, crooks, and pickpockets from both sides of the Sahara. To watch this scene is to give oneself some inkling of what it must have been like to be in a great medieval or classical city. Tourists are in a very small minority in Marrakesh and mostly, like us, pretty frightened people!

More typical, perhaps, of the medieval or earlier rural economy, are the very small country towns of Morocco which act solely as market centres. As one approaches one of these in the morning, one can see converging on it from country areas 10–20 kilometres around lines of donkeys or camels laden with many different kinds of produce – tomatoes, figs, grapes, oranges, eggs, salt, fowl, honey, goats. During the day there is much haggling and direct exchange, in which money plays a relatively minor role, and in the later afternoon the same pack-animals wend their way back into the hills and valleys with what they have bought or exchanged. The town here provides the location of the market and services – money changers, eating-places, hairdressers, a relatively small permanent population. There are also open markets at strategic points, which operate on certain days of the week; here too are the hundreds of stalls, rows of hairdressers, and purveyors of snacks, but with sundown all is packed away and the place is deserted.

The archaeologist observes with interest this socioeconomic life: the systems that underly what is being seen, the structures of certain kinds of site and activities and the patterns of rubbish disposal that result. Here the archaeologist is taking a rather different view from a socioeconomist. The latter will also be observing not only these relatively archaic ways of life, but also how they are changing (especially north of the Mediterranean) under the impact of western industrialization, notably the influence of motorized transport, new roads, cash-crops and tourism.

Subsistence

The agricultural economy can be studied in a wide variety of locations. The most widespread archaeological and landscape feature in all parts of southern Europe are the terraced fields, constructed at great expense of labour to build the revetment walls to retain the precious soil and facilitate irrigation, another major feature of classical and Arab farming. Although large areas of these are now abandoned, much more survive in use, yielding a wide variety of crops. Here can be seen in operation systems of small fields very like the so-called 'celtic' fields which until recently survived as earthworks so dramatically in the chalk downlands of southern England. They are rapidly now being bulldozed away for modern larger scale farming.

In arable areas, one can see ard-ploughs very similar to those in use in Iron Age or Roman Britain. They are being pulled by oxen (as in fourteenth century England) by donkeys, mules, horses, or camels, or even (in Morocco) very oddly by a camel and a donkey in tandem!

Sowing is still done in many areas by 'broadcasting' by hand from a basket (as in the Luttrell Psalter and the Bible), and reaping by hand, either by a sickle, or pulling the whole root out. All this is very labour intensive, as it was in pre-modern times in northern Europe. Threshing floors, a circular flat area, often with a retaining wall, are a very common feature still in Turkey, Greece, Spain and Portugal. The corn was broken up either by animals being led round and round the floor, or by animals pulling a sledge, whose front curved up, and whose underside was studded with sharp-edged flints or other stones. This *tribulum* is a direct descendant of the threshing sledge known by that name in classical times. We saw the *tribulum* at work in northern Spain

(Leon) and brought part of one back to York. It had been abandoned and thrown on a wood heap (we paid 100 pesetas for this, about 40p). We wedged it into the roof of the Land Rover and it now graces the hall of our department in York, where it can be studied at leisure.

Large areas of southern Europe are still given over to the olive and grape. The olive plantation trees, some covering thousands of hectares in mid-Spain, are said to be direct descendants of the Roman ones. The importance of wine in classical and medieval times can hardly be over-estimated; Mediterranean wine was being imported into Britain and Ireland from the Iron Age onwards (witnessed by finds of pottery *amphorae*) and one can still see the whole process of viticulture in virtually every European country south of Denmark.

Technology

I have already mentioned the threshing device, the *tribulum*, now being ousted by the threshing machine proper. Our main interests in the field of technology have been in irrigation, and in the related techniques of milling, the final process in the arable economy. Windmills and vertical-wheeled watermills are still to be found, though increasingly rarely in working order, in northern Europe, but *horizontal*-wheeled mills are different.

In 1972 I excavated one of only two Anglo-Saxon water-mills known in England, at Tamworth in the Midlands, and dated to the middle of the ninth century. Although the remains were relatively well preserved for such an ancient structure (due to waterlogging), we became interested in this primitive kind of mill, its origins and the exact way it worked, in order to understand our archaeological evidence from Tamworth better. This kind of mill now survives only in the southern Mediterranean and in the far north. It was to the south that we went in search of these. Our first field-work here was in Crete. We recorded details of several dozen ruined examples, but at last found two in complete working order, still earning their living grinding corn for the local community. Most of the mills we saw dated from the six-teenth–nineteenth centuries, but we had an invaluable insight into how such mills worked. We subsequently published a paper on the Cretan mills, and we have since then recorded horizontal-wheeled mills in South West France, the Pyrenees, southern Spain, the Canaries, and especially in northern Spain, in Galicia. Here, in a short tour, we found several examples still working, and this is probably the region where most still survive in Europe today, in an area where water is still very plentiful.

Another technology which was common in medieval Europe, but now survives in its old form only in the south is pottery-making, firing and selling. We have seen the entire process in traditional pottery-making areas in Spain and elsewhere, giving us an invaluable model for the medieval pottery manufacture in Britain.

Daily life

Peasants, and the peasant way of life, long extinct in northern Europe, are still common enough in the south. Electricity, plastics, TV, piped water and cars are rapidly changing country ways of life, but a great deal survives. One doesn't have to travel very far from tourist resorts to see grain being made into flour by a hand quern; butter being made by 'throwing' the buttermilk around in a bag made from a goat's stomach; shepherds in high mountains making soft cheese from goats' milk (using calor gas however!) and bringing their cheese down to the local market every Saturday; hand spinning, fulling and weaving; people milking animals by hand; using carts with solid wooden wheels; riding on pack-animals; and engaged in a wide variety of food-preparation and cooking. All of these activities are familiar to the archaeologist through the material debris they leave behind, and in these places one can see all details of the activities which produce such artifacts.

As a change from writing this book, my wife and I walk inland in the afternoons about a kilometre from the hotel where we are staying in the south Spanish province of

Almeria. Here in a small sheltered valley there are terraced fields, a threshing floor, a spring and washing place, a small gorge, palm trees, huge cacti. In this garden-like landscape are a group of four or five farms, mostly abandoned in the late 1950s and not yet taken over for white-stuccoed 'pueblo'-type villas of rich aliens.

The impression one gets from a recently deserted landscape of this kind is that this is what Britain must have looked like in the sixth century, with numerous ruined or semi-ruined buildings about, many of the fields reverting to scrub, hedges, revetments, water-supplies, and drainage neglected; and a marked demographic drop in rural areas. Oddly enough, the inheritors and improvers of the neglected landscape of Roman Britain and this part of southern Spain were the same people – the English – though for very different reasons!

In those farmhouses that have been abandoned, much of the material culture has been left behind, presumably because it is of such little value if one is moving to a new apartment block in a nearby town. Thus both houses and contents are still there, rather as if the inhabitants had died of the plague. We have made a plan of one of the farmhouses, and noted all the details of materials, construction and use of space; all the rooms have been numbered and the function of each worked out. We made an inventory of all the objects lying around in each room: iron-bound wooden chests, old broken chairs and tables, baskets, and other containers of sisal-weave; bottles, tins, ceramic dishes, a 'dead' bicycle, feather-mattresses, carved wooden beds, a string of garlic, hay, animal manure, a plough-beam and share, and many others. These objects of course belong to someone; they cannot be removed, only listed and photographed. Even if we don't use these data for any direct archaeological analogue, we are recording an example of material culture that will not survive where such farms continue in use, as modern materials fast supersede the old. This, it should be noted, is ten minutes' walk from one of the most popular tourist hotels on the south coast.

One of the archaeologist's most common finds is pottery, which has been made all over the world in an extraordinary variety of fabric, form and function. As already mentioned, we have studied pottery-making. We have also bought local ceramics in many countries in Europe. They now form at York a remarkable 'ethnographic collection', which we can use to illustrate to students the appearance of classical amphorae or medieval costrels, fish-dishes or jugs, for these things have changed very little.

Death and burial

This subject lends itself very much to ethnoarchaeology. For the archaeologist, the dead are one of the most important sources of evidence, for their skeletons, coffins, and grave goods. All these survive in varying degrees, but little remains of the wider aspects of death in society – the events leading up to the funeral, the funeral itself, and the major ripples in society that death causes. All these can of course be observed in modern society, to see what material remains might be found in favourable circumstances.

Death and burial is a subject that has received a lot of attention on a world-wide basis by archaeologists. From the earliest Stone Age burials through barrows, cists, tombs, burial ships, pyramids, cremations, to the millions of graves in cemeteries; from the richly-furnished jade-suited Chinese princesses of the second century BC to the modern public cemetery and the horrors of the American funeral industry, so well portrayed by Evelyn Waugh and Jessica Mitford.

One of my most successful (if rather ghoulish) lectures is on the 'archaeology of modern death', the material culture that surrounds death today from the infrastructure of the undertaking industry, with its flowers, hearses, and embalmers, to the funeral feasts and mourning dress and, especially, the rich source of grave memorials. I gathered the material for this lecture from many different ethnoarchaeological contexts. I have photographed a funeral in Sicily, 'cities of the dead', in the Mediterranean, the hundreds of clothed mummified bodies in the Capuchin crypt at Palermo, Islamic graves in Istanbul and the Atlas mountains, hearses in Spain, and funeral notices in Greece.

One of the best-known examples of ethnoarchaeology is the study of New England gravestones of the eighteenth and nineteenth centuries, which we have also photographed. Since every one is precisely dated, the patterns of changing form and symbolism in town and country areas can be exactly plotted. The changes from death's heads to cherubs to willow and urn can be seen in their beginnings in urban centres like Boston or Plymouth (where the 'fashions' arrived from Europe), gradually diffusing into country areas. This analysis gives a perfect model of the way such diffusion works, and has been used to check inferences about similar changes in form and symbolism in prehistory.

The wider our knowledge of modern death and burial, the more may we hope to understand the wide variety of mortuary behaviour we encounter in the ancient world. Why for instance do some people cremate, others bury, and yet others throw bodies in rivers or leave them out to be eaten? Why is cremation becoming more and more popular in today's Western Europe? What is the relationship between wealth and social status and the form or ostentation of grave or memorial?

Religion, ritual, and value-systems

This is too big a topic to deal with adequately in a short space. Archaeology is notoriously bad at being able to deduce the nature of early religious belief (we don't even know what Stonehenge 'means') or even much of what went on in people's minds. Comparative religion in the world today is very much a subject for anthropologists or theologians. All that archaeologists can do is to watch and observe and think – 'what would I make of all this if I found it in a ruin?' The reader is invited for a moment to be a Martian archaeologist excavating the ruins of our destroyed civilization. What would you make of a large building that is oriented east–west, that has no occupation dirt around it, and all the nourishment seems to be a bottle of wine and some wafers. There is a special table-like structure at the east end, and a sort of shallow bath on a stand at the other. There is a good deal of imagery of a rather violent kind, of someone nailed to a cross, etc. *We* know it's a Christian church and *we* know what all these things symbolize, but to an alien archaeologist it would be very puzzling. Hence our total incomprehension when faced with Indian or Far Eastern religious practice today, or even with Stonehenge.

On a more prosaic level, one ethnoarchaeological observation of religious practice did something to increase our confidence in the 'ritual' or religious character of a find some 1500 years earlier.

At Cadbury-Congresbury, in Somerset, we excavated a small pit of the sixth century AD, a 'Dark Age' site in Britain. In this pit was an odd assortment of bits of pot, metal objects, flints, slag, bone, glass waste, some 80 objects in all. It looked as if someone had deliberately gone round the site in the sixth century AD and gathered together a bit of everything that was around. Virtually everything we found in a large excavation was represented in this pit. Sealed beneath the rock lining were some weathered bits of human skull (there were no other burials on the site). Was all this 'ritual' (a word used by archaeologists when they don't understand what they have found)? If so, was it Christian or pagan (it could be either in this time and place)? Were the skull fragments something rather gruesome that the pit succeeded? Could we cite any ethnoarchaeological parallels for such a 'domestic assemblage' having a 'religious' interpretation?

The answer came soon afterwards when we were in a very remote part of Europe, the west coast of County Donegal in Ireland. Close to where we stayed was a holy well, part of an early Christian complex possibly itself more ancient. But the holy well was still, as often in Ireland, a place of Christian visitation. Around the little pool of water in a rock-cleft (which is all the well was) was an astonishing collection of objects – bits of clothing, combs, biros, a plastic magnifying glass, two religious tracts on holy water and happiness wrapped in paper bags, a collection of pre-decimal (valueless) coins in a purse; a hair-slide, and some more obviously Christian objects such as crosses and China Madonnas (one in a bottle). In a small cave close by were dozens more objects of the same kind, and bottles of all kinds from shampoo to detergent. In the mouth of the cave (which a small child might have crawled into) was a stone shaped like an old-fashioned bun-loaf, slightly anthropomorphic, but clearly natural. We photographed and listed these objects without moving them, classifying them by their material and original function. Discreet enquiry elicited the facts that all these objects were either associated with someone whose illness it was hoped to cure, or with someone who had been cured. The stone was a healing stone, used to effect a cure by being placed over the affected part. So potent was it, it was said, that it had been to America twice to cure Irish exiles. Someone had once thrown it into the sea, but it reappeared in the cave the next day. We later published all this as a piece of ethnoarchaeology of especial interest. It did not enable us to say that our sixth century pit *was* likewise a ritual feature, but it did show that it *could* have been. It wasn't entirely ridiculous to suggest that such a collection was religious, because we could now quote an *ethnoarchaeological parallel*.

In discussing the ethnoarchaeology of value-systems, we will look at rubbish and dirt. The English tourist in southern Europe is appalled by the way 'the locals' spread rubbish everywhere, especially in remote or beautiful country or coast areas. The wilder the place, the more one is likely to find dumps of plastic, glass and tin in places where there is no chance of it being collected by public garbage collection. In former times when most rubbish was organic it didn't matter so much, as it all rotted away. Now it doesn't, and the result to us is a major eyesore, not to mention the health hazards and dangers to children and animals. Our observation has been, however, that the locals *don't mind*. The wild areas are places beyond the areas that are useful – fields, bars, homes, gardens, work-places – and appropriate therefore for disposal of rubbish. Now that social custom has persuaded, for example the Spaniard, that the wild, especially the coastal spot, is a suitable place to drive to on a Sunday, some change might be expected, but it is not happening; they are apparently oblivious to it. It is part of their value-system, their attitude to dirt is not ours. Yet repeatedly we apply our own value judgements when we find dumps of dirt on floors, or round entrances, or down wells. We decide that this must be the work of 'squatters' rather than the 'proper' inhabitants, and start to think of suitable historical settings, of conquest or the collapse of political authority.

Finally, a piece of ethnoarchaeology that was not directly related to the past, but wholly to the material culture of present-day Christian centres: as part of our trip to northern Spain and the past-related agricultural and milling technology, we visited Lourdes and Santiago de Compostela. Although both these sites are important present-day pilgrimage centres, Lourdes in particular attracting over two million visitors a year, they are very different. Lourdes, in South West France is barely a hundred years old as a shrine, the site of St Bernadette's visions. Santiago de Compostela in North West Spain has been a pilgrim centre since the ninth century AD, and is the reputed burial place of St James. There are many other contrasts in the material culture, notably in the souvenirs sold for pilgrims to take home as witness of their visit. This is a custom that was very common in medieval times, pilgrim badges being worn on hat or cloak. That associated with St James is a scallop shell; this is the symbol all along the route, on signposts and other objects. The symbols for Lourdes are St Bernadette and the Virgin in the grotto of the visions. The souvenirs at Lourdes are an industry. The streets (but not the grotto) are more like Blackpool or Coney Island than a holy city. Every conceivable object that can be decorated with St Bernadette and the Virgin is sold in thousands, ranging from plastic bottles to collect the holy water to hats, from biscuits to household shrines, lit by electricity. They are sold in dozens of very vulgar shops with notices such as 'Tourisme et Religion'. We made an inventory and classification of the objects at both places (Santiago is much less obtrusive) rather as we had for the Irish holy well (Rahtz and Watts, 1985.)

The interest here is the extent to which such assemblages of the modern material culture of religions change. Earlier visitors to Lourdes described the vulgarity of the scene, but must have seen rather different range from those on sale in

1983. Similarly, a visitor in 2000 will find it interesting to compare our list with what is available then. Since Lourdes has been well documented from its inception by written accounts and photographs (not to mention all the commercial documents of account) it would be possible to relate all the changes to changing styles of pilgrimage, relative wealth, social habits, and especially available material, and develop archaeological theory accordingly.

CONCLUSIONS

I hope that all readers of this chapter will now go on their holidays with a more observant and less prejudiced eye, and will be able to avoid the boredom of the beaches. For our next chapter we turn to more light relief, the fringe areas of archaeology, perhaps suitable to be read *on* beaches as it was after all written on one!

7

Fringe Archaeology

'Archaeologists are a funny lot of people . . .' – well so they are, using the word in its 'odd' sense. They can also be quite funny in a humorous sense, and are certainly very jolly *en masse* at conferences and excursions. Individually they can also be humourists, but some are fearfully serious about it all. I adopt a jokey attitude towards archaeology, which to me is a kind of wider perspective. Archaeology, it might be paraphrased, is too important a subject *not* to be joked about. I also insert jokes into lectures as a way of keeping my audience awake. The trouble is that they remember the jokes, but not the rest of the lecture, so the jokes have to be *important* jokes which illustrate profound truths about something or other.

Archaeological humour can be at the expense of archaeologists. No-one has yet gathered up all the jokes about archaeology, though there are a few collections. Cartoons especially, in *Punch* and the *New Yorker* and elsewhere, are a valuable source for the study of changing social attitudes to archaeology. There are certain stock situations. One of the most common is the bearded 'professor' in shorts who is deciphering an inscription in an Egyptian tomb, only to find it says 'Kilroy was here' or variants. Other jokes concern people's attitudes to the past – the classic one is the soldier looking at Stonehenge across a barbed wire fence. 'Wot puzzles me', he says to his friend, 'is 'ow they got those stones over this 'ere wire'. Such jokes are funny because they embody major misunderstandings about the past. One of my favourite jokes, which I have told hundreds of times, embodies a profound contrast in philosophical attitudes, and neatly sums up the contrast between what archaeologists do, and what other people think they do:

Yorkshire farmer (to Oxford archaeologist digging in trench):
    'Ave yer found owt?' (for our non-English readers this
        is Yorkshire for: 'Have you found anything?')
Oxford archaeologist:
    (looking up) 'I beg your pardon?'
YF: 'I said, 'ave yer found owt?'
OA: (still puzzled)
    'Have I found out *what?*'
    (end of joke!)

There are also numerous jokes about Stone Age and Iron Age people, including regular comic strips (Asterix the Gaul, the Flintstones) which are compulsory study for anyone wishing to understand the mentality of our ancestors.

ARCHAEOLOGISTS' OWN JOKES

The humour that this chapter deals with is not, however, about that of the outside world, about archaeologists, ancient peoples, dinosaurs, ancient monuments, but those of archaeologists about themselves or their subject. It is thus introverted, esoteric, and exclusive. A major difficulty in writing this chapter is how to explain to the general reader what the jokes are *about*, to let him into the 'trade secrets' of archaeologists' humour. Much has been written on this subject in a general way, so I shall confine myself to a few personal examples, which I hope will be new to most readers.

HOW LIKELY IS LIKELY?

I begin by reproducing a short piece I wrote some years ago. It was written in half an hour as a fringe item at a local conference, but, because it expressed some fundamental truths *and* was quite funny, it was published. This short piece has been quoted more often than the major reports I've written, which is rather galling!

Modern archaeologists are constantly urging the necessity for a stricter and more scientific use of language and logic in archaeology. One of the more attractive facets of such thinking is that degrees of probability in the 'truth' of archaeological evidence might be quantified. There is much difference between the validity of, for instance, a date given by a coin sealed below a floor, and a date suggested for the use of that floor by the material lying on it. The first is a statement of fact, the second lies somewhere between 'possibly, though very unlikely' and 'very probable amounting almost to certainty'. Between these two extremes lies a range of quality of evidence which is infinite in its diversity both in kind and degree. Can the range be quantified? Windstrengths are given a ten-point (Beaufort) scale based on measurable characteristics. While archaeological evidence has more diversity than windstrengths, is it possible to erect a ten-point scale ranging from quality 1 (very unlikely) to 10 (certain), which can be linked with written equivalents?

We set it out thus:

Probability scale	Literary equivalent
1	very unlikely
2	unlikely
3	possible
4	very possible
5	likely
6	more than likely
7	probable
8	very probable
9	virtually certain
10	certain

Does the table illustrate the absurdity of a mathematical probability scale of the range of written terms commonly used in archaeological reports? The latter seems to me to be more than likely (scale 6). The more 'elegant' archaeological reports are littered with dozens of different phrases used to express subtle nuances of degrees of probability. Are they used as sober assessments of the evidence or as elements of rhetoric to persuade the reader to one subjective opinion on what the evidence can bear? If there is no such thing as 'objective evidence' from an excavation, then these phrases will carry a double message: 'this is what I think the evidence was in the ground, and this is what I think it implies.'

The use of a scale might force archaeologists to think more carefully about what weight the evidence will bear. Too often, the choice of the elegant phrase covers up a vague and woolly approach to the evidence; in the best of hands it will of course express half-tones of delicate balance between this and that which simply cannot be quantified. This is a valid technique if its object is to direct the reader's attention to the evidence itself, a challenging invitation to him to decide for himself just how likely is the claim made.

Unfortunately few writers of archaeological reports are skilful in the use of words, even if they do in fact fully appreciate what can and what cannot be deduced from the evidence in the ground. If they do not have the gift of words, they might do better to use a number scale; their readers would then at least know how likely *they* thought was likely!

Even worse, some writers are more concerned with converting readers to their point of view than expounding a balanced estimate of the validity of the evidence. To do this, they use literary techniques which are misleading or even dishonest in a 'scientific' report. They do in fact create an *inverse* scale of probability. Discerning readers will see through this, and apply a reversal factor; others will be persuaded. Examples of such an inverse scale might run thus: (the 'modesty' of the first example is as misleading as the persuasiveness of the rest).

Phrase	Actual meaning
'just possible'	I'm pretty certain but I can't actually prove it; the reader will see how cautious and clever I'm being
'there is some evidence pointing towards . . .'	there isn't any but it would be nice if there were
'the evidence suggests that . . .'	if it were twisted beyond recognition
'it is reasonable to suggest that . . .'	it is unreasonable but I may persuade my readers to believe it by an appeal to their reasonableness
'virtually certain'	I'm on very shaky ground here
'there can be no doubt that . . .' (or more commonly) 'doubtless'	anybody who disagrees will feel a fool
'plausible'	well, ever so interesting if it were true
'it would be premature to suggest'	but wouldn't it be fun
'all the evidence taken together points to . . .'	it all points in different directions
'obviously' 'indisputably' 'presumably'	there is no actual evidence
'reference to the section'	no-one is likely to do this, I hope
'no right-thinking scholar can doubt' or 'the discerning reader will observe . . .'	these are my final trump cards

It would be tedious to document the examples given above (I can't be bothered to do it).

These dubious phrases about the quality of evidence should put the discerning reader on his guard, but an ability to 'translate' other statements found in archaeological reports is also needed, for example:

Phrase	Actual Meaning
'further research may indicate . . .'	mine certainly doesn't
'adverse excavation conditions . . .'	the recording was terrible
'there was no evidence of . . .'	if there was, we didn't see it
'the object crumbled into dust on exposure to the air . . .'	Joe sat on it
'the relationship between these layers was uncertain . . .'	Joe dug it away when we weren't looking
'examination of the section showed that . . .'	we didn't see it in digging on one side of the baulk anyway after it had been doctored with a trowel
'the site was excavated by open area method . . .'	just as well, as no one could check the sections
'the levels above the mosaic floor consisted of infilling of soil and stones . . .'	we missed 7 periods of post-Roman occupation
'there was evidence of squatting . . .'	we missed 14 post-Roman periods
'although little survived to suggest a post-Roman occupation . . .'	we bulldozed the top ten feet
'the date of the end of the occupation of the villa was shown by the latest coins, which were of Honorius . . .'	I don't believe in all this Dark Age nonsense
'a scatter of small stones associated with two handmade sherds . . .'	I do
'it was not possible . . .'	we didn't think of it till afterwards
'a flimsy structure . . .'	Moira planned the post-holes it can hardly have stood up on its own
'a pot scatter of uncertain date . . .'	we wrecked the site

THE END OF ROMAN BRITAIN

One short piece was written directly for inclusion in a lecture on 'The End of Roman Britain', because I could think of no better way of making a point, and making it memorable (alas!) by personalization. The point was to expose a major fallacy found in much archaeological writing about this period. This is that the dating of the latest levels in (say) a Roman villa is given by the dating of the latest coins found in that deposit, or by the date of manufacture of the pottery found. Since coins ceased to reach this country very soon after *c*. AD 400, and Roman pottery manufacture did not long survive this breakdown in a monetary economy (if indeed it hadn't already run down before then), these objects can only give a *date after which* the latest occupation took place, which might be 50, 100 or 200 years after those dates. At a conservative estimate, there were 20 million pots in use in Roman Britain in AD 400; they didn't all get broken in a resounding smash soon after that date; and those that survived became even more valuable.

A related fallacy is that when archaeologists find that the latest levels are full of 'dirt' – bones, potsherds, oyster shells, dead dogs, with fires being lit on mosaic pavements – they (if they are Roman archaeologists, who believe 'proper' people lived cleanly) attribute these remains to 'squatters', rather than to long drawn out secondary usage of the building by people with different life-styles or purposes. These points are brought out in the following bedtime story:

Marcus, a late Romano-Briton, was living in an urban environment in AD 400 with his wife Calpurnia and their two young children Festus and Priscilla. Discussion round their dinner table was similar to that of today – impending doom and a feeling that civilized life as they knew it was not going to survive the adulthood of their children. Marcus was already remarking that the pottery stalls in the market were not so packed, or with so much variety as they were when he was a boy, and his grandfather had told him that what pottery there was lacked the elegance of earlier days. He had indeed inherited a samian bowl, but it was never used, being now an antique and kept on a shelf and showed round only on ancestor day.

After a few more years had passed, he returned from the market one day with the news that he had not been able to buy a new black-burnished cooking pot which Calpurnia had asked him to get. He'd been told by old Sextus the pottery-stall keeper that he hadn't been able to get any – they weren't making them any more – it was getting too difficult to market them and there was no profit in it. They looked round somewhat ruefully at the rows of pots on the kitchen shelves, which had suddenly acquired a new value. 'You'd better not break any more', he jokingly told her. They counted them up – there were 35 of them of various sizes from dish to storage jar.

By AD 420, 20 had been broken, both by the clumsiness of the ageing and arthritic Calpurnia, but also by her lively grandchildren; and now that it was clear that the potters were not going to resume production, each loss occasioned a terrible family row.

By AD 440 both Marcus and Calpurnia were dead, and the house and pottery had passed into the hands of their son, Festus, now himself approaching middle age, with two grown-up children. Because of their increasing rarity value, the breaking rate had dropped; five more pots had gone by AD 440, leaving ten surviving.

Twenty years later, on a dark November afternoon in AD 460, the now aged widower Festus was sitting by the fire, dreaming of the old days of central heating by hypocaust which he dimly remembered as a boy. There was a noise outside the back door and then it suddenly burst open, and two uncouth hairy toughs stormed into the room, gabbling in some guttural tongue. Old Festus jumped up and protested, but was silenced by a mortal blow. The intruders knocked down everything in sight, the samian bowl smashed on the floor, and so did the other ten pots. The old man staggered away to die, and the toughs set fire to the house after eating all the food they could find.

Fifteen hundred years passed, and an archaeologist began work on this area. He found the broken pottery on the floor, and noted in his diary that this was clearly the 'behavioural residue' of the latest 'squatter' occupation of the house, albeit rather 'squalid' (since the invaders had left chicken bones and oyster shells of their last meal on the floor too). When the dig was finished, the archaeologist studied the pottery and looked up parallels for fabric and form. Surprise, surprise, they were all mid- to late-fourth century – the samian was of course 'residual', whatever that means. In the report we duly find 'the final phase was rather squalid; the associated pottery dated this occupation to the later fourth century, a conclusion confirmed by the coin sequence in the area, which also ends with issues of Valentinian II and Honorius' (late fourth century).

THE ALTERNATIVE ABBEY

My next example of 'in' humour derives from our excavations at Bordesley Abbey. In some dirt in the choir area of the church, we found a small ivory die (plural dice). This immediately conjured up ideas of gambling within the church during long boring masses, and of generally lax discipline in the monastery. The idea was rather reinforced by finding chicken bones in the dirt under the choir-stalls: a surreptitious snack. Out of this, in the teatime break, grew a whole alternative scenario – a life at Bordesley Abbey which the abbot didn't know about (unless he was, as some medieval abbots were, more degenerate and corrupt than any of his monks). This was 'realized' on a blackboard by Ian Burrow, an inveterate archaeologist/joker, and although it was ephemeral in this form, I did luckily take a photograph of it. I later realized that it could be used to illustrate in a memorable way what we mean when we talk of the contrast between the

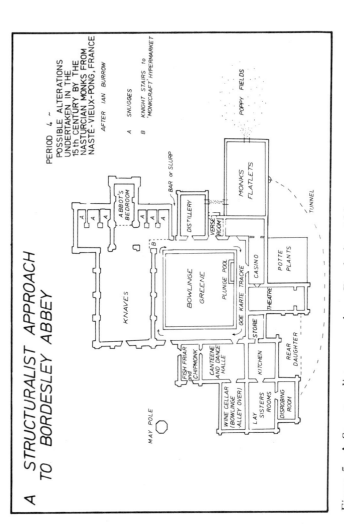

Figure 5   A Structuralist approach to Bordesley Abbey.

way institutions *appear* to operate, the 'public' image, and what goes on in reality, a matter of interest to both sociologists, anthropologists and archaeologists. Figure 5 was the result.

As a postscript to this, I read in the *Statistics* volume in this series (Kennedy, 1983, page 57) that dice were used by medieval monks to help them decide which virtue should be specially practised that day; so we had probably maligned our Bordesley monks.

DARK AGE NAMES

From the same stable came figure 6. This arose out of a general debate about whether Dark Age archaeology should be studied as *archaeology* independent of the difficult and controversial written sources, or whether, as Professor Leslie Alcock believes (and argues for in a highly scholarly way) the understanding of the archaeology can come only from a full study of the texts, and be interpreted within that framework, that is, with reference to named historical figures, places and dates. Thus we find frequently in Dark Age archaeological or historical writings the adjectives *Arthurian, Patrician,* and *Gildaic,* referring to Arthur, Patrick, and Gildas. All we've done is add a few more. This was done, not because we believed in such a framework of study, but quite the reverse. We were, by making fun of it, trying to discredit it. We were at that time digging a hillfort at Cadbury-Congresbury (CADCONG). Leslie Alcock was at that time digging another Dark Age hillfort in Somerset (Cadbury-Camelot) and there was friendly rivalry between the two Cadbury excavations. We were really poking fun at the Arthurian and Camelot associations which figured so largely in the fund-raising and media publicity of the 'other' Cadbury dig. I should hasten to add that when Leslie visited our dig and saw the diagram on the wall of the excavation hut, he was very amused. The reader will find the sources for this principally in Gildas (*De Excidu Britanniae*) and the *Anglo-Saxon Chronicle*. This diagram is also a satire on the general archaeological habit of naming periods, which applies equally to prehistory as to the Dark Ages.

DATE	PERIOD			PHASE	SUB-PHASE
400		R		PRE - GERMANIAN	Honorific
	S				Wansdyckensian I
		O		GERMANIAN	Pelagian
					Auxerrian
	U	M		PRE - ARTHURIAN	Ambrosian
					Superbian
			A		
	B			ARTHURIAN	Merlinian
					Amphoric
			N		
500					Badonic
		R			Camelottian (PSEUDO - ARTHURIAN)
	P			GILDAIC	
		O			Pacific
	O				Sodomic
		M		CONGERRIAN	
	S				Sarumaniac Barburic
			A		
	T				Dyrhamic Wansdyckensian II
			N		
600				AUGUSTINIAN	
	S				Avalonian
	A				
	X				
	O				
	N				
					Pencil Wooden

Figure 6 Dark Age CADCONG – a tentative chronology.

HUMOUR IN THE HISTORY OF ARCHAEOLOGY

Much archaeological humour, including the above examples, is a product of its day, and may quickly become dated, like

Punch cartoons of the 1870s. It does nevertheless have some relevance in the history of the archaeology of the period, a social by-product of a kind which it would be difficult to infer from the academic publications of the same period.

Some of the items above verge on fantasy (to put it mildly) and are also perhaps related to science fiction. This can also be humorous, but has a potentially more important role, which will be discussed in the next section.

SCIENCE FICTION AND ACADEMIA

Science fiction is now a respectable academic topic. One can get a degree in it in at least one American institution, and my own university recently ran an open course on the subject, organized by Dr Edward James, who combines interests in history and archaeology with a strong involvement in SF; the lecturers considered the relationship of SF to history, language, sociology, theology, science, and pseudo-science. They demonstrated the ways in which SF was able to bring a new dimension to each subject; the lecturer giving 'SF and Theology' (Ian Watson) claimed for example (and very plausibly) that SF had done more for comparative theology in its explorations of alternative gods than had the academics in theology departments.

THE IMPORTANCE OF ARCHAEOLOGICAL SF

Archaeology did not figure in this series, but there is no doubt of SF's importance here in expanding the horizons of an archaeologist's mind, even more than the ethnoarchaeology discussed in Chapter 6. No-one has yet surveyed the whole field of archaeology in SF, and this book is not the place to do it. All I can do here is to indicate briefly the modes of treatment archaeology has had or might have from SF writers. Most of that written is relatively uninformed, and little has been written by archaeologists themselves.

SF is a remedy against parochialism, anthropocentrism and

too easy cultural assumptions. One criticism that can justly be made of this book is that, because it is so much about my own experiences, it is very Rahtz-centric; much archaeology practised in Britain is Anglo-centric, or at best Europacentric. The archaeology of the Far East, Polynesia, America, Australia or Africa is hardly known to most British archaeologists or students. Most archaeologists, however, are anthropocentric (perhaps by definition?) though this is now being remedied by a greater awareness of the interdependence of man both on and with other species and of both with the natural environment. All archaeologists, however, who are not into SF are *terra*centric. The *Journal of Galactic Archaeology* has yet to reach its first issue, owing to the dismal failure of our astronauts or space probes to find living or dead civilizations on the moon or other planets. They can so far only be invented in SF. Some critics of archaeology suggest, however, that some of the hypothetical models put out by archaeologists themselves border on SF.

A letter to the *Times Higher Education Supplement* in 1980 deplored the use of its pages for SF. Reading on, I was amazed to learn that the writer was referring to me. I had written a piece for the THES in which I summarized the advanced archaeological techniques which could and should be tried out in the new excavations at Sutton Hoo (Chapter 8), which it is hoped will set new standards of methodology. Although the techniques I was suggesting had already been used somewhere or had been shown to be *theoretically* possible (if expensive), the letter-writer thought I was talking in SF terms. He suggested I should be deep-frozen until some time in the future when such techniques were possible. The Sutton Hoo debate inspired a short piece of actual SF, lampooning me (reproduced here from *Rescue News*, March 1980).

Following a nationwide appeal involving press and television the nation has been persuaded that excavations at Sutton Hoo are inevitable. Sufficient funds were raised to carry out six months' rescue excavation in advance of the construction of a humidity/temperature-controlled, rabbit-proof Archaeodrome. The builders, working from suspended walkways so as to avoid disturbance to the site, constructed this revolutionary structure in at least three years at an estimated cost of £75 million.

The excavation will undoubtedly be a major achievement for British Archaeology, and the team is undergoing intensive training in the use of the Microtrowel. This revolutionary new tool facilitates the extraction of single grains of sand, records their positions in three dimensions, the information being fed directly into the bank of computers which is currently being installed on the first floor of the British Museum, now renamed the Sutton Hoo Museum. The excavation is to be televised and extracts will be transmitted to viewers all over the world. . . . Professor Ritz explained that they would have preferred to move the whole site to the Museum before excavation began. This is a well-known technique: one simply drives a metal sheet underneath the site, and then lifts it off in one piece. Ultimately the site will be transferred by special transporter, after each grain of sand has been carefully labelled and packed. On the basis of the excavation record the sand grains will then be reassembled as the Museum's centre-piece. Dr Morbid-Fret and his team are to be deep-frozen so that their long experience will be available to assist in the reinterpretation of the old excavations.

MODES OF ARCHAEOLOGICAL SF

The modes within which SF and archaeology have been or might be created may be listed as follows; they are of variable academic interest, or usefulness to archaeology:

(1) Terran archaeologists (that's us) investigating the remains or extinct civilizations on other worlds (or even the ethnography of living communities, of giant spiders with red

eyes on stalks). These are very common in SF; even Captain Kirk occasionally includes an archaeologist in his team chosen to beam down.

The academic point in such studies is to explore the extent to which archaeological method and theory are *universally* (sic) applicable to the study of material culture anywhere; or only on earth, to the creations of *homo sapiens sapiens*. Biologists would certainly see the basic approaches of their discipline as applicable to any life-form, and so too should archaeologists. SF offers scope here for the development of abstract archaeological theory.

(2) Archaeologists from other worlds examining the remains of our (life-extinct) culture. This is much easier, because we are familiar with the material culture they will find. The interest here is in the extent to which objective archaeological approaches will get it all wrong. We have already seen a real-life example of this by Terran archaeologists (see Millie's Camp, pp. 88–9). There are some excellent pieces in this genre. One of the most famous appeared in the *New Statesman* many years ago – an investigation of the ruins of the London Underground. This was entirely interpreted in ritual terms: the Line and Circle folk lived in this complex labyrinth with its rigid symbolism. At intervals there were special enclosed booths, in each of which was a ritual instrument linked by a wire to a special box, in which offerings could be made through slots.

One of Arthur Clarke's best stories concerns the reconstruction of hominid Life on Earth based on a surviving artefact buried deeply in a time-capsule below fused concrete – a Walt Disney cartoon of Donald Duck. In David Lodge's *The British Museum is Falling Down*, it is suggested that the distribution of Roman Catholic households could be plotted by the incidence of broken thermometers used to determine the safe period for pious housewives. In a full-scale illustrated book, *The Mystery of the Motel*, a motel room is found preserved intact, even with its door-hanger 'Do not Disturb'. Inside are two skeletons. One lies on a ritual couch frozen in death while gazing at a glass-fronted box, which apparently used to transmit messages to the faithful (not far

120

out here!). Another skeleton was lying in a larger porcelain ritual receptacle, while close by was a smaller one with a hinged seat, and a long piece of paper in a roll on which to write one's thoughts. Reproductions of the latter receptacle in miniature were seen being sold on the site as souvenirs.

The point in all these is just the same as in Millie's Camp – what can we make of archaeological evidence if we don't know anything of the cultural background of the people whose remains we are studying? What are the *ways* in which we can get it wrong? This topic has recently been explored in relation to a body of evidence which had already been fully published in a conventional way (Rahtz and Watts, 1983). *The Martian Expedition to Wharram Percy* (Fahtz, 1985) finds a series of stones close to a large non-domestic building. By analogy with others elsewhere which say 'Here Lies . . .' (the Martians have been studying Earth for some time and know the basic framework of English), it is assumed that the stones cover burials, but nowhere is this explicit at Wharram – the purpose is clearly a memorial one. But the dead are there; Hon Jurst, the director of the expedition, has found Terran skeletons under the nearby building. Demographic data are worked out from information on the stones, with the assistance of a document dug up in the ruins of nearby *Eboracum* by the expedition's historian, Boris Meresford. The expedition, however, is defeated in trying to work out the religious beliefs of these Wharram Terrans. What is this place, Jesus, where someone goes to sleep? 'Heaven' seems to be a prize, awarded to those who do well. There are also quotations from one 'Mat', in archaic English of some centuries earlier. The author, Rilip Fahtz, had a serious purpose here: to determine what the stones really told us as artefacts, independently of what we knew about nineteenth- and twentieth-century culture and beliefs in England. This kind of study is 'distancing oneself from one's data', avoiding cultural bias in the observer.

(3) SF interpretations of archaeological evidence. This gets dangerously close to space fantasy, or the literary devices of historical novelists; and to the heresies put out by Von Däniken and his kind. An example here is Pierre Boulle's

Monkey Planet, in which future Terran archaeologists play a crucial role in showing that the planet had been occupied by humans before the great apes. In this category, too, come several stories of space-travellers landing on earth, surviving, degenerating and becoming the first hominids in our fossil record – an alternative creation myth.

(4) The reconstructions of a past which have an eye to the future. These must be distinguished from the wide field of total reconstruction of the past, using all available archaeological historical material (for example, *Asterix* or William Golding's *The Spire,* 1964) or where such data have even been totally ignored (e.g. the film *A Million Years BC*).

There has to be some hint, explicit or otherwise, that the past people being reconstructed are conscious of future students of their life-style, notably of archaeologists looking at their material culture. There is some suggestion of this in Angus Wilson's *Anglo-Saxon Attitudes* (1956) (compulsory reading for all archaeologists) or in Golding's *The Inheritors* (1955). The idea is more explicit in the numerous jokes/ cartoons, about the deliberate 'fooling' of future archaeologists by creating patterns of artefacts that are not 'unconscious'. There is scope for much writing here, not only in the abstract, such as a scene where early people are depicted behaving in this way and talking about it, but where the actual finds of today (such as the Sutton Hoo ship-burial, or Stonehenge) are explained by reconstructions of elaborate past hoaxes (as the relics of Piltdown Man proved to be).

(5) Time-travel. Archaeologists who can travel in time and/or space clearly have a big advantage when it comes to cross-cultural, diachromic, or trans-spatial comparisons between different societies. Most of these restrict their travellers to Earth (except Dr Who; see also the end of the film '2001'), and rather sadly to contexts already partly known from history. Thus, the tourist time-travellers in Silverberg's *Up the Line* (1969) want to go back to see historical events such as the crucifixion or the sack of Constantinople. Because these are so popular, different couriers and their parties encounter each other in the milling crowds (the couriers even encounter *themselves* on successive

visits). In another book in this genre (Kilworth, 1975), the crowd of time-travelling tourists help in the crucifixion, thinking that they are thus blending in with the crowds of Jews and Romans; but in fact there isn't a crowd of Jews and Romans, there are only tourists.

Similarly Mark Twain's classic *A Connecticut Yankee at the Court of King Arthur* is limited in its archaeological or historical appreciation of sixth-century England by a nineteenth-century American, but is a splendid essay in crosscultural comparison. More imaginative is Robert Westall's *The Wind Eye,* a children's classic in which a modern professor and his family sail into the mist off the Northumberland coast, and become involved in the world of St Cuthbert, lovingly delineated with an eye to archaeological and historical detail, and very evocative of the Farne Islands.

There is much room for new writing here in visiting older societies and seeing in the technology and material culture now being excavated parallels to our own world and checking our hypotheses; or even in the abstract concept of reversible time, where we are in fact encountering the future in order to predict the past (Eh?).

(6) Archaeologists as part of inter-galactic societies. Reconstructions of other societies sometimes include archaeologists, as in the first volume of Asimov's *Foundation,* or in the *Hitch-Hiker's Guide to the Galaxy* (Adams, 1979). They serve as a useful device to SF writers to develop the *history* of other worlds.

THE PURSUIT OF TRUTH

We have seen in Chapters 2 and 3 that the academic and highminded pursuit of the truth about the past is not the mainspring of motivation for most archaeology. The desire for truth is not by any means universal, even if the concept of truth, or even the truth about any particular topic, *could* be universal. This is just as well, as disputes about the 'facts' of the past in archaeology or history, and their interpretation, provide the principal material for scholarly debate. Even so, among academics there is a general agreement that the common aim is to get as near as possible to finding out what did happen in the past, and why it happened, even if the latter was not at all clear to the people to whom things were happening.

For the great majority of people, the facts about the past are not of any great interest. They are concerned more with how the images conjured up by history or archaeology can be used in their own imagination, or even perverted to support theories. Leaving on one side most of the non-academic motives for archaeology listed in Chapters 2 and 3, such as its use for political manipulation, we now concentrate on two, the use of archaeology to support religious belief, and to support myth. It may be difficult to disentangle these two: one man's religion is another man's myth.

Here I want to concentrate on the apparent dislike of scientific truth or at best the inability to decide what is scientific. This is a turning away from rationalism and from basic concepts of logic. Although most of my examples will be semi-humorous (because to laugh at anything is often the best mode of attack – my text is really derision), I do find the lunatic fringe of archaeology highly distasteful. Distortion of the truth or even the suppression of it is the antithesis of all I believe in, and directly counter to my own aims in doing and teaching archaeology. The lunatic fringe may seem to be harmless eccentrics, but to me they are as potentially danger-ous to human society (even if they have the best intentions) as the other perverters of truth, the tyrants and dictators. I will first examine the reasons why people like irrational things related to archaeology, and then illustrate some with examples, drawn from a vast field. In the final section I will give a case-study of Glastonbury. Here I can speak with some authority, as I dug there for six seasons in the 1960s.

THE MAGNETISM OF THE IRRATIONAL

People reject scientific truth for several reasons:

    (1)   A dislike of science, logic, and reason, because they

are associated with scientific, logical and reasonable people, who our Group 1 find irritating and inhuman, lacking 'normal' passions and emotion; notably schoolmasters, scientists, statisticians, and others in authority. These make our Group 1 feel inferior and ignorant, because they find it difficult to see the difference between common sense (which must be true because it is rooted in everyday experience) and anything which is not easily understood.

(2)   An attraction towards the mystic, hidden 'real' truths, not accessible to those who need proof or a reasoned argument. Truths of this kind are known intuitively to poets, artists, saints, gurus, mystics, drug-addicts and 'primitive people'. Such knowledge was 'of course' formerly part of the common heritage, but it has been 'lost' in the development of civilization, and can only be recovered in non-scientific ways. There is an organization in Britain devoted to this search – RILKO – 'Research into Lost Knowledge Organization'.

(3)   A belief that science and reason are actually evil, in that they are often opposed to religious belief, which is based on faith, not reason (though many great scientists and other scholars seem to manage to live in both worlds). The Oxford Laboratory recently received a letter accusing them of promoting evil in that they were, in their new radio-carbon dating work, seeking to overthrow the word of God, as represented in a literal interpretation of the Bible. Evangelical Christians the world over are seeking to discredit radio-carbon dating, especially when, as in Australia, it supported an antiquity of 40,000 years for the 'inferior' Aborigine (Chapter 2), though in the next breath, he will be a relic of the time before man was made in the divine image.

(4)   A liking for the romantic, which is believed to be more interesting and exciting than bare historical truth. If King Arthur didn't actually exist, he should have done. Archaeologists and historians who discredit Arthur, or the story of Alfred burning the cakes, or rape and pillage Vikings, are 'spoilers', depriving the common man of his cultural heritage. Exotic explanations are more palatable than boring archaeological ones. The prime evidence for this is the colossal sales of Von Däniken's books, and the rather more

respectable sagas of Thor Heyerdahl. Von Däniken sought to show, among other things, that many of the most striking monuments of the past had been built with the help of earlier spacemen. A South American relief sculpture was interpretated as a representation of such an extra-terrestial visitor, looking very much like an American astronaut, complete with space-suit and bubble hat. To the eternal credit of the BBC they devoted a two-hour programme to a detailed exposé not only of Von Däniken's failure to observe elementary laws of evidence and logic, but also to his having resorted to suppression or downright fraud to bolster up his fantasy. The sad thing was, as the BBC hammered home, that far from restoring to the people their lost knowledge, their true cultural heritage, he was in fact depriving them of it, by denying to man the great achievements of art and great stone monuments which his ancestors created without the help of God or spacemen. He was denigrating man; but man does not seem to mind – he goes on buying the books.

(5) Irrationality provides a free-for-all platform. Since there are no rules, anyone can win. The 'expert' is no longer top dog ('experts baffled' is a favourite among journalists). Who can gainsay that a thing is possible? that two or three coincidences make a fact? Everyone can be his own savant, and nobody need feel inferior any more – you don't have to have a university education to arrive at intuitive proofs.

LEY–LINES

One of the best-known examples of current irrational archaeology is that of ley-lines. To be a ley-liner you take a ruler and pencil and join up all the 'ancient features' on an Ordnance Survey Map. If any four of them are in a straight line, you have found a ley-line. The lines mark the courses or paths of 'earth-energy'. These were well known to Neolithic man, who, like ley-liners, could 'feel' the line. They could store the energy in henge-monuments. This knowledge was 'lost' in the decadent age of metal.

There are no limits to the kind of places you can put on

your line. One may be a hedge line, another a Bronze Age barrow, another a church, another a tree – the idea is that there is a continuity in time of these spots being utilized. You can of course in this way find 'ley-lines' which join up anything in any direction. The whole argument has been carefully, systematically and sympathetically exploded by Tom Williamson and Liz Bellamy (1983).

DOWSING OR DIVINING

These are much more respectable techniques. Diviners, using a variety of similar devices such as wands or forked sticks of wood, plastic, or metal, can and do find water, water-pipes, metals and other buried things. There may well be a scientific explanation for the slight reaction of the human body to buried features which makes itself manifest by a muscular twitch which causes the apparatus to move vertically or horizontally. While this cannot yet be demonstrated scientifically, it does work. Farmers and oil companies pay diviners money to seek the presence of oil or water. A recent academic study in Northumberland has made a strong case for the ability of an experienced diviner to recover the plans of long-vanished walls of early churches (Bailey, 1983, Briggs *et al.*, 1983). Dowsing on the ground may be acceptable; what the rationalist finds harder to swallow is divining on *maps,* which is clearly moving towards the paranormal world of psychic phenomena. The diviner may well be a useful adjunct to the archaeologist's battery of ground-sensing devices (as is the metal-detector in the right hands). It can, however, lead to pure fantasy of the most dangerous kind.

AMERICA'S PAST

We have already mentioned, in Chapter 2, the varied motivations of American archaeology, one of which is the search for their roots. In the lunatic fringe here much effort is expended in proving the case for non-indigenous pre-Columbus visits or even colonizations, by Phoenicians, refugees from drowned Atlantis, the lost tribes of Israel, New England Celts, ancient astronauts, Vikings, and Prince Madoc the Welshman.

Fantastic claims are made for patently faked archaeological finds such as the Kensington 'rune-stone', and the Vinland map (Davies, 1979, see also *Antiquity*, number 210, March 1980, page 69, for an excellent review, and Reynolds and Ross in earlier issues in 1978 and 1979, together with a whole series of witty exposés by Glyn Daniels in many issues of *Antiquity*.)

Commercial interests capitalize on public credulity. In North Salem, New Hampshire, there is a site called Mystery Hill, 'America's Stonehenge – 2000 BC'. This is a 20 ha complex of stone buildings, walls, wells, drains, and other features, including a 4½ tonne granite slab on stone legs. The structures have been attributed variously to Irish Culdee Monks about AD 1000, to 'megalithic' immigrants of about 2000 BC, or (probably more realistically) to Jonathan Pattee between 1832 and 1849. Archaeoastronomy is also dragged in: 'it can now be stated that Mystery Hill is, among other things, unquestionably a calendrical site able to determine solar and lunar movements with utmost accuracy.' . . . 'slabs with strange markings' . . . 'translated as being of ancient European Scripts' . . . 'more work must be done . . . before the inscriptions will be accepted by the academic community'. All this falls hardly short of fraud, and should be discouraged by the USA tourist authorities. It is an insult to the American public, to the indigenous Indian, and to Pattee.

OTHER WONDERS

One of the most persistent quests in archaeology is the search for Noah's Ark on Mount Ararat in Turkey. The Secretary of the General Council of Seventh-day Adventists said in 1964 that he was convinced that pieces of wood brought down from 14,000 feet up on the mountain, were part of a giant boat (two-thirds of the size of the *Queen Mary*). There were several hundreds of tons of wood under an ice pack; the timber was tooled and it was a type of oak so hard that electrical blades had been broken in cutting it. In 1965 the *Daily Telegraph* published an air-photograph of another ark on Ararat, 400 feet long. Geologists, however, dismissed the shape as having been caused by erosion of volcanic rocks about a million years ago.

In England we have the Druids, who meet annually at Stonehenge at the Midsummer sunrise, an occasion which draws spectators of such dubious habits that the police have to be there in force. The Chosen Chief of the Druids told the Heretics Society in Cambridge that the most reliable method of finding out about Stonehenge was to go there and 'lie down and let the past and its true meaning seep into one's body and bones'.

Many more examples could be quoted of the sad world of alternative archaeology, but all pale before the Mecca of all irrationality: the sacred Isle of Avalon, Glastonbury, to which we will now wend our sceptical footsteps for a detailed case-study.

GLASTONBURY

The present small town of Glastonbury in Somerset is part of a promontory which protrudes into the low-lying and marshy areas of the Somerset Levels extending to the Bristol Channel. Although there is a neck of land above flooding level connecting Glastonbury to higher ground to the east, its appearance as an 'island' is accentuated by a striking steep hill over 150 metres high. This is Glastonbury Tor, a very prominent landmark which can be seen from up to 30km away. The area is very rich in archaeology. As early as the fifth millennium BC there were early Neolithic settlements in the Levels, on small drier areas, linked by well-carpentered wooden trackways, found excellently preserved in the peat, with many artefacts of the same period. Many further trackways of later millennia have been excavated, and in the centuries just before Christ there were marsh-edge settlements here, very well known as the 'Glastonbury and Meare Lake Villages', one of the richest and best preserved and most extensively excavated archaeological sites in Britain. There are many finds at Glastonbury itself of Roman date, indicating the presence of a villa on the lower ground.

In my excavations on the summit of the Tor, I found wooden buildings and finds of the sixth century AD, including pieces of pottery from the Eastern Mediterranean (see Chapter 3 for some discussion of these). The site might have been the stronghold of a Dark Age chieftain, or an early ascetic monastic site.

In the later seventh or early eighth century, a monastery with an important church was founded on the lower ground and received much support from the Anglo-Saxon kings of Wessex and England. Dunstan was its Abbot in the tenth century. Several satellite monasteries were established in the eighth or ninth centuries; these included one on the Tor, of which I excavated what may have been the timber church and a few rock-cut cells. Another was at Beckery, on the edge of the marshes, where I excavated the whole church and cemetery (Rahtz and Hirst, 1974).

In the Middle Ages, Glastonbury flourished. A church of St Michael was built on the Tor, whose tower crowns it to this day. The Norman and later Abbey was one of the richest in the land. Its Abbot, Richard Whiting, was hanged on the Tor by Henry VIII's officials at the Dissolution in the sixteenth century, it is said for refusing to reveal the whereabouts of the Abbey treasure.

After the Dissolution, Glastonbury declined. The Abbey was destroyed and most of its stone was carted away, leaving only some still impressive ruins today. The site was acquired by the Church of England in the earlier part of this century (to the annoyance of the Roman Catholic Church, who have of course a much better claim to it) and there are now annual Christian festivals, pilgrimages and other events.

One might think that all this archaeology and history was exciting enough to stir anyone's imagination. Glastonbury has, however, during the last fifty years, but especially since the 1960s, become the magnet for an incredible variety of hippies, weirdos, drop-outs, and psychos, of every conceivable belief and in every stage of dress and undress, flowing hair and uncleanliness. How has this come about? We may point to several reasons. The striking natural topography and the long religious associations have attracted those who seek enlightenment in a Christian context. The main lure has been some 'alternative archaeology' of the distant past. The medieval monks, in their efforts to make Glastonbury an important centre of pilgrimage and to attract wealth, made extravagant claims about the antiquity of the Abbey. They produced documents which purported to show that Joseph of Arimathea had come to Glastonbury after the death of Christ, and had brought with him phials containing the blood and sweat of Jesus. William of Malmesbury, writing in the twelfth century, records what the monks told him, though he may have been sceptic as to their truth. They also, at the end of the twelfth century, claimed to have disinterred the body of none other than King Arthur, in a deep grave, in a dug-out coffin. With him was a lead cross on which was inscribed HIC IACET INCLYTUS REX ARTURIUS IN INSULA AVALONIA (Here lies the famous King Arthur in the Island of Avalon.) This lead cross that they claimed to have found survived to be drawn and published in the seventeenth century. Modern academic opinion, but by no means unanimously, believes that the whole of the documentary evidence, and that of the grave, was a total monkish invention with no basis in fact.

From the twelfth century to the present day the Glastonbury legends grew. Guinevere with long yellow hair had joined Arthur in his grave. The visitors to Glastonbury now included not only Joseph, but also Jesus Christ, brought as a boy by Joseph on an earlier trip to get tin; part of his schooldays were spent at the Druidic College at Glastonbury where the best education in the world could be obtained. To these were added Mary the mother of Jesus, and even Mary Magdalene. The accretion of legends have become fact in the minds of the credulous Avalonians. The Chalice Well is still believed to be the place where Joseph deposited the phials (though my excavations there proved the 'well' to be a medieval well-house, built around a spring to safeguard the water supply to the Abbey, and gradually buried in silt). It has been written that its structure displays Egyptian influence, because the Hebrews in their bondage were obliged to build in the Egyptian style. The well is used to support the statement that the Tor was an observatory. This was 'self-evident from the fact that there was a well at its base, for the wells were the telescopes of the ancient astronomers'. A flowering thorn bush on a nearby hill called Wirral was Joseph's staff planted when he arrived, crying out (in English) to his party (to explain the name) 'Friends, we are weary all.' Another story of course has Joseph bring the Holy Grail, a wooden cup. King Arthur's grave is still shown to visitors in the grounds of the Abbey.

This is not all, however. One of the most remarkable claims about the area in the 1930s, was that the hills around bore the signs of the zodiac. These were outlined by hedge-lines, banks, roads, lanes, tracks and any other lines that could be invoked (rather like the ley-lines discussed above). They could be traced out on maps and on air-photographs, and were published in full by the late Katherine Maltwood (1935, 1937). The zodiac still has many supporters, but the fallacious basis of the evidence on which it was delineated was discussed in a dispassionate and scientific way by Ian Burrow in *Popular Archaeology* in 1983 (February, number 4(8)).

The Tor itself has attracted its share of legends. Two ideas that still persist in Glastonbury are (a) that it is an artificial mound (b) that it is hollow inside. A more credible theory was put forward by the late Geoffery Russell, and taken up and elaborated by Geoffery Ashe (1979), who lives at its foot. This is that the Tor is a kind of three-dimensional maze, of which the 'paths' are formed by an arrangement of terraces around its steep slopes. The pattern postulated – a widespread symbol – is similar to many other mazes such as that on the floor of Chartres Cathedral, or Cretan coins, on a pillar at Pompeii and many others. The conventional explanation of the terraces is that they are natural (the result of the differential erosion of the varying strata of which the Tor is

made) or that they are strip lynchets (for medieval agricul-
ture). I am sufficiently open-minded on this one to have said
in print, 'The argument is complex, but is worth consideration . . . if the maze theory were demonstrated to be true, it
would clearly be of the greatest relevance to the origins of
Glastonbury as a centre.' I would still stick to this. Such
technology as the 'sculpting' of a hill would not be in any way
beyond the capacity of Neolithic man, who we know was
settled in the area; and the models made by Geoffery Russell
do look quite convincing.

The Tor is also a centre of witchcraft. I was visited on my
dig there by an exotic lady who claimed to be their Queen (of
the 'white' witches). We had an interesting conversation,
during the course of which she told me, among other things,
that we were digging in the wrong place (?). We found rather
unpleasant evidence of witchcraft practices beneath the
church tower, and had an unpleasant experience with a 'black'
hypnotist on the Tor. As I was writing this chapter, I was
rung up and told that the caller had found a black granite
gravestone on the Tor recently, inscribed G C in odd letters.
He took this to be Guinevere of Camelot, and suggested that
there might be important graves below, including that of
Jesus Christ. I have not yet been to see the stone.

In the light of all this, it is hardly surprising that Glastonbury attracted very large numbers of young people in the
1960s in the world-wide movement concerned with seeking
new values in an evil world, a movement that had its origins
in America and spread through Europe to Katmandu and the
Far East. The Love People and Flower Power are part of
social history now, but their impact on Glastonbury in 1969
was immense. Something of this was expressed in words
which I cannot hope to emulate, by Jon Pepper (*Guardian*, 20
December, 1969); I quote from his article:

'The Hippie Vale of Avalon'

The frosts and fogs have come to Avalon. The deep,
brooding mysteries still cling to the vale, even more so
in the present melds of haze and wintry sunbeams, but

the 1969 Children's Crusades to Glastonbury in search
of the town's strange enchantments have finally ended,
defeated by the cold. The fields are now empty of their
tents and flutes. The place has sunk into a thankful
hibernation. . . . Predictably, however, while the tents
of the new visitors have dotted the hillsides, they have
crossed the townspeople.

The arrival of the pilgrims – and the cult of
Glastonbury which now looks well set among the Love
people – has led to paroxysms of righteous horror from
some of the town elders, particularly the trustees of
the Chalice Well, whose holy, healing waters have
apparently been used for communal ablutions. Of
course, the intruders cannot do anything right: half the
town acusses them of being unwashed and an affront
to civilisation, while the other half berates them for
washing their jeans, shaving and sprucing up in the
Chalice Well Waters. . . . For the young Utopians,
however, Glastonbury, as one devotee has written, is
strong magic. Muz Murray told me: 'It's my contention
that the Tor and the giant zodiac imprinted on the
landscape round Glastonbury which has had enough
written about it now to hold some veracity, were
together the centre of cosmic power in Atlantean days.'
. . . Clearly, Glastonbury is crying out for deep
examination. A group of academics and writers calling
itself the Research into Lost Knowledge Organisation
are now trying to do just this. So far they have produced
learned but empty-ended reports. Full aerial reconnaissance of Glastonbury, archaeological excavations of the
Tor, and a massive concentration of cooperative intellectual effort from the appropriate university departments aimed at sorting out the real wood from the trees
ought to be undertaken!

Apart from the confusion of academics with RILKO, the
sad thing about this is his plea for archaeological excavations
on the Tor! I *did* excavate the summit in between 1964 and
1966 (Rahtz, 1971), but clearly as this was 'scientific' and only

found 'archaeological evidence' our (quite epic) effort remained unnoticed, even so soon after as three years.

Glastonbury still has many visitors, and inspires visions in people. One lady came to see me from California. Although she had no previous background knowledge of Glastonbury or its legends, she had a series of visions of underground chambers in one of the Glastonbury hills. These were very clear and explicit 'just like a coloured movie', she later told me. She was so disturbed and obsessed by then, and her husband got so worried about her, that they spent all their savings (14,000 dollars – they were not wealthy people) to come to Glastonbury. They had heard of my work in Somerset, and came to see me first where I was then digging. There was no doubt whatsoever of her sincerity. She produced a series of drawings which she had done from memory which were very detailed about what would be found in the underground chamber. I set her on the road to Glastonbury, and although she had never been to England before, she unhesitatingly identified Wirral Hill as the scene of her vision, and pointed out where excavation would locate the chamber. She was naturally very disappointed that archaeological resources were not available to test the truth of her vision, but she returned to America satisfied at least that she had seen the right spot. The experience she related is by no means unique, but the only one of which I have had first-hand experience.

Finally in this study of Glastonbury we may look at the history of excavations there, which are quite a saga in themselves. The first excavations were in the Abbey grounds, in the shadow of the great ruinous fragments of the complex of churches. This was in the years following the acquisition of the site by the Church. Two or three directors were involved in the work, which was not of very good quality, and was never fully published. The last of them in this first campaign was a remarkable figure, Frederick Bligh Bond, an architect and mystic. Like many others at that time and since, he believed that the Abbey site was the earliest Christian nucleus in Britain, the seat (as we have seen) already of a Druidic College in prehistoric times. As one of the Glastonbury faithful said to me, 'Christianity was already present at Glastonbury in the first century BC; it was only waiting for Christ's birth to be given its name.' Bond accordingly looked for evidence that would prove these earliest associations, including (as he believed) the plan of a circular monastery (a church in the middle, and cells round the edge of the circle). In his search for this and other important early features, he claimed to have had guidance by spirit writing from a medieval monk of Glastonbury, who told him exactly where to dig. Not surprisingly, the Church disapproved of his unethical approach, and in 1921 closed the excavations down precipitately, to quote Bond 'without warning and before my measurements could be taken'. Bond retired to America.

In 1937, Bond had plans to resume work, backed by American money, and sponsored by Sir Charles Marston. But war came; in 1945 Bond returned to Britain to die, and Marston died in 1946.

A new initiative was begun in 1952 with the same American backing; the desire of the sponsors was still to find evidence of the earliest Christian settlement. The new director was, however, an archaeologist of international reputation, Dr C. A. Ralegh Radford. He pointed out that in modern archaeology one could not just dive down to the earliest levels, but one had to deal carefully with the Saxon and medieval structures that lay above. Ralegh Radford made important discoveries between then and 1962, but these, like the earlier excavations, have not yet been published in detail, so it is difficult at present to assess the significance of what was found.

My own involvement began in 1962 at the invitation of the Chalice Well Trust, and its Chairman, W. Tudor Pole, who was introduced to me by Ralegh Radford. Tudor Pole was a remarkable man, another mystic, who believed in reincarnation. He himself could remember three previous existences. The first was in the first century AD, when he was present at the important events in Jerusalem. The second was in the seventh century when he worked in the library of the Great Palace of Constantinople. He once showed me a list of all the books there, which he remembered. He in fact took part in the excavations there in the 1930s, perhaps hoping the library would be found. The third existence was as a cardinal in the fourteenth century AD. He is well known for his books on spiritualism and especially for the book he wrote jointly with the famous novelist Rosamund Lehmann, concerning her daughter Sally, who had died young in tragic circumstances.

Tudor Pole understood archaeology, but clearly hoped that I too would find evidence to support the early legends. I was commissioned first to dig at the Chalice Well, with the results I have mentioned above. Then there were my three seasons at the Tor, and later two at Beckery Chapel. Though the archaeological results were of the greatest interest, I had not perhaps found what was hoped for. Tudor Pole never expressed dissatisfaction or disappointment – he knew I was finding all that was there, but some of his disciples were not so complimentary. One said, 'Mr Rahtz, I can give you three reasons why you haven't found anything: (1) You're digging in the wrong place' (in this she agreed with the witches' Queen); (2) 'You're digging at the wrong time'(?); and (3) 'you're the wrong person' – I really couldn't win!

Glastonbury illustrates the enormous gulfs that separate the aims, methods and expectations of the scientific archaeologist from those who seek lost knowledge. Is the gulf as wide between the archaeologist and the general public? In my last chapter (9) we shall look at this public, which includes you, the reader, and ask what archaeology means or could mean to them and to you.

8

Two Case-Studies in British Archaeology

INTRODUCTION

These two studies, Sutton Hoo and Wharram Percy, have been chosen because they are both well known outside Britain, both have a long background history, both are highly significant in their own field, but are different from each other in almost every other respect. They are also projects of which I have some personal experience. They illustrate many of the concepts and problems that this book has dealt with.

SUTTON HOO

Earlier work

This is a cemetery of burial mounds on a terrace at the edge of cultivated land overlooking the estuary of the River Deben in Suffolk. Although there is prehistoric occupation on the site, the fame of the site lies in its Anglo-Saxon connections. It is believed to be one of the burial places, if not the principal or only one, of the kings of the dynasty which ruled East Anglia in the sixth–seventh centuries AD. This claim rests partly on a number of isolated finds from robbed-out mounds, but principally on the results of a remarkable excavation which took place there in 1939. The then owner, Mrs E. M. Pretty, decided, partly at least from active curiosity, that she would like the barrows on her land opened. She entrusted the work to Ipswich Museum, and they to an archaeologist of some local reputation, Basil Brown. In 1938 he partly excavated three mounds with only minor results. In the fourth, opened in 1939, he very soon came across the remains of a ship, of which only corroded clench nails, soil discolorations and textural differences in sand were still present. The uncovering and photography of this ghost of a ship in 1939 was quite a *tour de force*. He quickly realized that it was a burial-ship, which had not been robbed in antiquity.

News of the discovery got to the then Office of Works, who invited Charles Philips to take over. He organized a small team of the leading archaeologists of the day, and they assembled on the site at very short notice. It was August 1939, and war was only a month away.

The burial deposit was immensely rich and important; it was worth many millions of pounds, and its bequest by Mrs Pretty to the nation one of the largest such gifts ever made. It is remarkable, looking back from half a century on, that usable records were made at all. The team did not even have an excavation hut, and the astonishing finds of gold, silver, and many other materials were packed for despatch to the British Museum in moss. Once the richness of the deposit was realized, strict security had to be maintained.

All was safely stored away by the time war broke out. It was many years before the British Museum could begin the work of conservation and publication. Between the fifties and the seventies this was entrusted to Rupert Bruce-Mitford, who has now published three great volumes on the ship-burial. He also directed a re-excavation of the mound in 1965–1971, to clear up outstanding problems and to take a plaster cast of the boat.

Although no actual body was found, probably because of the acid conditions, the mound is generally believed to have been the burial place of King Redwald, who died *c.* 625, a man of power and fame in his day. Readers who have not seen the Sutton Hoo finds should without delay visit the British Museum, where they are splendidly displayed.

The new initiative

My case-study is not, however, about the 1939 excavation and its long aftermath, but is about the new excavations which are now being done there. I shall look at the long process of planning that brought this new initiative to fruit; the legal, financial, academic, personality and other problems that had to be overcome; the structure of the sponsoring and controlling organizations; the aims of the work; the new methods being used, and the preliminary results up to the time this book goes to press. This background should prepare readers for a proper appreciation of work taking place there in 1985 and later years, and its exposition by the BBC and elsewhere. Nothing could be more different in aims, organization, and method than the 1939 excavation and the present campaign.

The successive interim and final publications of the ship-burial had already inspired a great deal of learned comment from archaeologists and historians, especially those in Britain, Scandinavia, and Germany. Many new problems were posed, many new questions were asked. It was generally agreed that many of the problems raised could be answered by further work in the field. We knew a lot about one mound, and a very little about three others, but virtually nothing of the cemetery as a whole, or its immediate area, or its regional context within East Anglia. Many believed that further digging should be done, but there was also a big faction who were against it, for reasons discussed below.

Rupert Bruce-Mitford was, however, convinced that further excavation and fieldwork were matters of high priority in British archaeology generally, and he approached me in 1978 to discuss ways in which we might further the project. We formed a small steering committee, which included Rosemary Cramp, Barry Cunliffe, and Robert Pretty, the son of the 1939 owner; he had retained the 'archaeological rights' in the land, and also wanted to see more work done.

Now began an uphill battle which took four years to win, and which generated for me alone three box-files full of paper. Discretion precludes a frank and honest *exposé* of the details of the saga, though the papers will be splendid material for the historians of archaeology and of archaeologists in the next century! Suffice it to say here there were many problems connected with personalities and institutions: this is nothing new in archaeology.

First there was funding and sponsorship. It was generally agreed that the British Museum with their great resources and expertise should be a major sponsor. The Society of Antiquaries also wished to support a major new research project. In the end, our small steering committee was absorbed into a joint committee of the SOA and BM, with generous support from the National Maritime Museum (who were interested in further data on boats), the BBC (who saw here the material for a splendid TV series) and the Suffolk County Council. Their archaeologists, notably Stanley West and Keith Wade, had for some time been working on the wider problems of the area, and their participation was essential. Two committees now control the project – a small executive committee who deal with the action needed, and a larger, more representative one which meets once a year to hear and comment on reports of results.

By no means everybody agreed, however, that *any* work should go ahead. Many objectors were vociferous in their opposition.

The great debate

The debate may be summarized by tabulating the arguments put forward by those opposed to the work, followed in each case by our response.

Objection A. The site is a safe one, not subject to the hazards of ploughing, or of motorway, quarrying or other development; it has a measure of legal protection. Excavation is by definition *destruction* of the monument. It is the duty of this generation to preserve monuments, and the archaeology contained within them, not to destroy them. The longer Sutton Hoo is left, the better. Each successive generation uses better techniques and recovers more data than its predecessors. We are trustees for those that come after. Unlike endangered species, historic sites cannot reproduce themselves, each one is unique. The site should be given extra legal and physical protection. (This is the familiar Rescue *verses* Research debate.)

Answer. The site is not safe. Rabbits, moles and bracken are destroying underground evidence. Two-legged predators armed with metal-detectors are rife in the area. As recently as 1983, ploughing encroached on the edges of the protected area. In 1982 a large hole was dug in the centre of one of the shallow unexcavated barrows to a depth of over a metre, into the subsoil, by person or persons unknown: it was unkindly suggested that *we* had dug it, to 'fake' a threat. The local rumour was that it had been dug, not by treasure hunters, but as a 'hide' by duck-shooters. While it is true that each generation does better and better archaeology, what is the point of preserving data if it were *never* to be realized? Who will decide when the time has come? Each generation has a right to dig at least *part* of such a crucial site. Excavation is not destruction of the *monument*; any mound can and will be restored to its former appearance after excavation. The monument will be much more interesting and educational because of the extra understanding that archaeology has provided. How are techniques to be improved if not through prestige projects like this one? One of the avowed aims of our work has always been to use Sutton Hoo as a 'test-bed' for new techniques of prediction, excavation, recording and analysis.

Objection B. Sutton Hoo is exotic and unique. While this makes it attractive to museum sponsors or the BBC, it is not really in the mainstream of British archaeology, which should be concerned with the broader patterns of ordinary human settlement, not with the burial-places of kings. The resources which it is planned to direct into Sutton Hoo (perhaps half a million pounds in five years, in the first instance) could more profitably be deployed in a dozen other equally worthwhile, but less exotic Anglo-Saxon projects. Publicity given to the Sutton Hoo project will encourage the mistaken belief that archaeologists dig for treasure not knowledge.

Answer. While exotic and unique sites are not ones on which to base general theories of settlement development, they are an important part of it. A case can be made academically for understanding as much as possible about the highest level of Anglo-Saxon society, its barrows and other burial places; such problems can be answered *only* by excavations of this kind. The massive amount of scholarly writing generated by the 1939 discoveries is witness to widespread academic interest in this kind of archaeology, in this country and abroad. There is a need to expand the 1939 data-base, and to put its content into a wider context, both in relation to the cemetery itself, and in its local and regional setting. The resources available for Sutton Hoo will *not* be available for any other project, being private research money; only a site like Sutton Hoo could attract such funds in sufficient quantity. It is in the interests of archaeology as a whole that public interest in the past *is* stimulated, and how better than by excavating a site that is already famous? Mounting a controlled scientific expedition at a site where public expectations are of glamorous finds and treasure is the best way of educating people to the real meaning of archaeology. It is easier to put over modern archaeology to a public that is 'captive' and already excited (even if initially for the wrong reasons). In Sutton Hoo there is uniquely a coincidence of academic and popular interest. Through the BBC, site tours, the local (Woodbridge) museum, and other ways, it will be possible gradually to replace the excitement already present in the public at the prospect of treasure, by the alternative excitement of the understanding of Anglo-Saxon culture, archaeological method and complex explanation, all carried out in a highly professional and responsible way.

Objection C. Whatever the sponsors may say about their high-minded and academic approach their motives are suspect; they are really after more 'loot' like that found in 1939. This is especially true of the British Museum, which constantly seeks to enrich its collections. The project is elitist in conception. There has been no full and open discussion either of the aims of the project, or of the methods appropriate to its execution.

Answer. 'Loot' is not the primary objective of the project, though further finds of high quality would undoubtedly help to put the 1939 objects into a better context. Understanding the cemetery as a whole, and its immediate surroundings, is the primary aim. There has been extensive publicity of the project; a session was specially arranged at the 1979 Anglo-Saxon Cemeteries Conference at Oxford on Sutton Hoo, where I set out the pros and cons (Rahtz, 1980), and where opinions were invited, to be included in our published report on the conference. The few that were received were all in favour, and were subsequently published. There was no point in presenting a full research design at that stage, before the details of funding and management had been fully worked out, and before a director had been appointed. An important feature of the work is to be extensive field-work in the area, with the collaboration of the Suffolk County Council, to find out as much as possible of the whole Anglo-Saxon settlement pattern. Finally the excavation will not embark on any major barrow until all earlier partial excavations of robbed mounds have been completed, the site has been made safe, and as much as possible found out about the site as a whole by every known prospecting device.

Legal problems

The reader may wonder why, if the project is to be funded by private money, there has to be so much time and effort (and space in these pages) devoted to answering the arguments of objectors whose money is not being spent, as would be the case if this were a publicly-sponsored and financed excavation.

The reason is that Sutton Hoo is a scheduled site, protected by law. While it is difficult for legal protection to be enforced against rabbits or human burrowings (or even an airport or motorway, if such were to be planned to cross the area) it can be invoked to prohibit even scientific and highly respectable excavations. Under recent legislation, applications for consent to excavate a scheduled site will be given only if there is 'no serious objection from informed academic opinion', and that the proposed work is 'in the public interest'. In the case of Sutton Hoo, academic opinion was clearly not unanimous. Objectors can force a public enquiry.

Current work

Most objectors were satisfied, for the time being at least, at a public meeting in London in April 1983. Much of the credit for this must go to the then newly-appointed director of the work, Martin Carver, who in a witty and stimulating lecture made the whole project demonstrably exciting and important, as well as giving it a sound ethical and methodologically impeccable basis.

Carver's degree was in general science. He is also an ex-military man, like other great archaeologists before him (including Wheeler). Like myself, he entered archaeology late. In his case this was through a graduate course at Durham. During the 1970s he made a name for himself by his work in urban archaeology, making substantial and imaginative contributions by excavation and writing to Durham, Lichfield, Stafford, Worcester, and Shrewsbury. He has also been successful in integrating a field unit into the archaeology course at the University of Birmingham.

On appointment, his initial task was to prepare a research design. This comprised a detailed proposal of the aims of the project, the programme of work planned, the timing of each phase and a detailed costing. Such documents, while common enough in commerce and industry, are still rare in archaeology, but such management skills are increasingly important and should form parts of all archaeologists' training. He has also given lectures at most universities, and has done much to allay misgivings about the aims of the project. He has also published a preliminary *Bulletin* (Carver, 1983), incorporating the research design and setting out the background to the project's work:

> Although a further harvest of valuable objects is not anticipated, (and does not form any part of these objectives) the burial assemblage from mound 1 the British Museum has undoubtedly won, through its beauty and vivacity, many new friends for archaeology. It is perverse to disdain objects which are universally admired, such admiration should rather be transformed into understanding, and this the project aims to do.

The regional survey is left in the hands of the County Council, through its field archaeologists West and Wade, in close association with Carver. But the principal expenditure of resources will be on the site itself, and its immediate locality of the Deben estuary. Carver's strategy here is divided into two parts: *evaluation* and *excavation*; these will be accompanied by campaigns connected with site management, publicity and education, and the regional study of the Sutton Hoo area and the Anglo-Saxon kingdom of East Anglia. Martin Carver has been active in travelling round the country, seeking commercial and academic help, in cash and in kind (a lawnmower manufacturer, for instance, supplied a machine free of charge for the initial cleaning-up operation). A series of academic seminars is also being held at the Universities of Cambridge, East Anglia, Oxford and Birmingham on such themes as Anglo-Saxon kingship; the kingdom of East Anglia; state formation in North West Europe; princely burial; barrow cemeteries in England; cemetery forms in the fourth–eighth centuries AD; paganism and Christianity in the seventh century; concepts of wealth in archaeology; and methodological seminars on intensive remote sensing (pre-excavation mapping), 'site geometry' using electronic survey systems and computerized graphics, and chemical enhancement of opaque soils.

Site evaluation. Following the initial work described above, the first phase of evaluation began with the collection of all

the extant records and photographs, which have been transferred to a computerized archive. Woodbridge Museum
stimulated local interest by an exhibition to illustrate past,
present and projected work. A member of the museum staff
turned up a previously unnoticed newspaper cutting from
the *Ipswich Journal* of 24 November 1860. 'One of five (*sic*)
Roman (*sic*) mounds was opened!' Two bushels of 'iron screw
bolts' were recovered, presumably clench-nails from a 'ship-
ghost'. They were taken to a local blacksmith, to be made
into horseshoes.

In the field, Carver's execution of his design began with
clearing the site of all undergrowth – bushes, bracken, and
other coarse growth. This was done in the Autumn of 1983
by a team supplied by the local Borstal (a remedial penal
institution for young offenders) who have since undertaken to
keep the site 'shaved' and therefore much more visible. This
enabled a new survey to be made, which identified over 200
former disturbances. These included recent treasure-hunting
holes; previous excavations; anti-glider ditches dug in the
1939–45 war; a water-pipe trench; quarrying for golf course
bunkers; and disturbances by tanks, who found the mounds a
rather exciting course for practice in the war; the site was also
used as a 2-inch mortar range. New air-photographs were
taken, which revealed the presence of at least one unrecorded
barrow, now virtually flat but showing up as an area of
differential grass and other vegetational growth. Metal-
detectors were used to clear the area of live shells and other
debris of the wartime use of the site. Predictive mapping
of underground features was then begun, using electrical
resistivity survey, fluxgate gradiometer and magnetic sus-
ceptibility, and ground-penetrating radar-pulse survey. All
these will help to obtain the maximum data on the site before
excavation is begun.

Finally, a guard was posted; one of the team slept in a
caravan on site. A raid by four men in a car, on Christmas
Day 1983, was scared off.

In work currently in progress, a vegetation survey has been
mapped, and a detailed contour plan made by electronic
distance measurement. Experiments are being made with a

viscous compound which it is hoped will consolidate and prevent the erosion of the soft sand, which forms the subsoil of Sutton Hoo and is the principal constituent of the barrows. It will also hopefully enhance the different colorations of the sand, to enable the stains of coffins, bodies, ships, and former wooden features to be seen more clearly.

An area of 1000 square metres will be covered in black polythene and left for a while, so that the grass mat will die, and can subsequently be removed and cleaned with the minimum of disturbance. The surface underneath this will then be sprayed with the viscous compound, so that its whole surface can be mapped to gain maximum information before digging. Outside the barrow area, in the nearby ploughed area and wood, trial cuttings will be made to see if any archaeological features extend beyond the known limits of the site.

Some of the old excavations, such as the trenches cut through other mounds by Basil Brown in 1938, and the anti-glider ditches, will be emptied. The soil will be sieved to see if any important finds were missed, to enable a study to be made of the sections thus revealed, and also to see if modern methods can detect any additional details of stratification.

Environmental studies will look at pollen, beetles, snails and flora from both buried and present surfaces. There will also be subaquatic exploration of the River Deben opposite Woodbridge, as it is believed that the boats were taken to the site by this route. The work may not only find possible landing places or structures, but also determine the natural topography and environment of the estuary edge in earlier centuries.

It can be seen that these evaluation exercises will maximize our understanding of the site without any 'destructive' excavation, and allow the testing of some new and important techniques in dealing with sand sites, in excavation and recording, through chemistry, and electronic and computer development.

Excavation. On the completion of the evaluation exercises decisions will have to be taken on how much, if any, of the site should be excavated, and the grounds on which legal permission to excavate must be sought. The aims of further digging would be quite specific. One would be to determine the order in which the barrows were constructed by careful examination of the areas where their edges intersect using, for example, soil colour enhancement techniques. If these will have been proved effective, a second project would be the total excavation of the barrows trenched by Basil Brown. The objective here would be to examine the structure of the mounds to see if tip-lines, etc., could be discerned (to explain how the barrow was built) and also to recover all evidence from these partly destroyed barrows. Depending on the outcome of all this work, further excavation would include a zone of the cemetery, including mounds and the areas between. These various options plan to leave some part of the site intact for later generations.

In all this work, priority will be given to site security in the short and long term, and to involving the public in a programme of explication and education. Apart from the important involvement by the BBC (who have already filmed the evaluation exercises), there will be exhibitions, lectures, and site tours. One innovation in both excavation and public presentation will be the use of continuous colour video monitoring. This will be invaluable in providing 'action replays' of important stages of the excavation for the archaeologists; but it will also be used to give visitors a close-up view of the actual digging, as if they were looking over the excavator's shoulder. The image can also be transmitted by landline across the river to Woodbridge where visitors can see a continuous live coverage of what is happening on the dig. As the work progresses, there may be exciting developments (if funding allows) in such techniques as total excavation cover (inflatable buildings with constant light, temperature, humidity and pressure); overhead gantries on which can be hung electrically movable 'cradles' on which excavators can recline, to avoid exerting any pressure by their weight on fragile deposits (perhaps space technology can provide us with a weightless atmosphere so that archaeologists can float around the dig!); freeze-drying on site of crucial deposits so that they can be lifted and transported to a laboratory for dissection; mechanized ways of removing spoil from the site (and bringing it back for site restoration); and developments in three-dimensional colour photography and computer simulation (see pp. 118–19 for a satire on this).

Sutton Hoo is an exciting prospect, and it is hoped that this account will alert readers to follow the progress of the work through the press and TV.

(see pp. 118–19 for a satire on this)

WHARRAM PERCY

Earlier work

Wharram is in a fairly remote area, 40 kilometres North East of York, on the high chalk of the Yorkshire Wolds, some 30 kilometres from the North Sea coast. The project is concerned not only with the now deserted village of Wharram Percy, but with a wider area of other townships, and with the neighbouring parish of Wharram le Street.

The site is well known in British archaeology and beyond as a deserted medieval village. It is one of many hundreds of such settlements which were flourishing at various times in the Middle Ages, but which were abandoned for various reasons. These have been categorized as, for example, desertions due to the Cistercian monks who 'cleared' rural areas to secure their solitude; to the creation of royal forests for hunting; to the long-term results of fourteenth-century plagues (the Black Death); and to changing economic circumstances, such as the rising price of wool as against corn, which made it possible to run a tract of land with one shepherd, where previously a whole community was engaged in tilling the land.

Not surprisingly, such sites are of great interest to medieval economic historians, and it was one of these, Professor Maurice Beresford, who was the first person to dig at Wharram in 1950. He was attracted to the site because there were very well-defined earthworks, and fairly good medieval documentary sources. He was not an archaeologist, and he dug simply to show that the earthworks did represent medieval peasant buildings. He was interested too in the question of when the village was deserted. He was joined by a Cambridge-trained archaeologist – John Hurst – in 1952, and they have continued to collaborate on the site for well over 30 years. Since 1980 I have become archaeological codirector with Hurst, so we are now an elderly triumvirate.

Although Wharram began as a medieval village excavation, it has expanded its aims and questions out of all recognition, both in space to include the neighbouring areas (and beyond in some topics) and in time back to the end of the Ice Age, and forward to the present. These changes have not come about as a result of a structured developing strategy, they are the result of chance discoveries and reflect also changes in the aims of medieval archaeology. Indeed Wharram can be seen as a microcosm of the development of rural medieval settlement studies during these decades. It has also become well known for the methodological developments that John Hurst has pioneered there, notably that of area excavation, as opposed to the 'grid' or 'box' system developed by Mortimer Wheeler. The essential difference is between a *horizontal* approach – seeing all of one layer at a time – and Wheeler's *vertical* approach, that of studying sections through several layers. The reader is referred to Barker (1977) to understand what this means technically.

Wharram is a research excavation. For the first 20 years, it was run on a shoe-string budget of a few hundred pounds a year. A band of faithful diggers gathered there each year, paid their own expenses, and gave their help free. This built up a great *esprit de corps* which now extends into the third generation. In 1974, however, Lord Middleton, the owner, generously gave the site to the nation. It became a 'guardianship' site, one of a small number of British sites which are safeguarded from all threats, and for which the new Historic Buildings and Monuments Commission takes responsibility.

The effect of this change was twofold. Firstly, the site now had to be made available for the public to see, as an 'ancient monument'; it had to be maintained, displayed and explained. Secondly, as a result, all excavation, while still research (with few exceptions such as tree-planting threats), was also geared to finding out more about the site, so that some well-preserved structures could be 'laid out' for the public to see, and so that it could be explained to them in an intelligible manner. This is a great challenge. Wharram is not immediately attractive as an ancient monument in the way that castles or abbeys are; there is little to see beyond a ruined church and its churchyard except grass-covered humps and bumps. These mean little to the layman unless they can be explained.

The new conditions also meant more money; the budget is now several thousand pounds a year, which enables senior staff to be paid. But the work-force, numbering over a hundred at peak times remains mostly volunteers and students. Money is also put into consolidating the church, labelling earthworks by concrete and metal plaques, and (in 1983) the re-creation of the medieval fish-pond by building a new dam across the stream. The outlines of peasant houses that have been dug are indicated by stone slabs, and the plan of long vanished parts of the church is shown by marked-out areas of turf, stone, and gravel. Today, in 1985, the site is increasingly attracting tourists, and has a high educational value. There may soon be a site display centre, and perhaps, eventually, even a resident custodian.

The site

The Wharram site covers a large area, a sheltered valley with a stream running through it, and a windswept terrace or plateau above it. In the valley are the church and churchyard (with its memorial stones) the medieval and later vicarages, two watermills (known from written sources) the medieval fish-pond, and an eighteenth-century farm. Of the latter three joined cottages survive. These were lived in until *c.* 1960, but after that became the excavation headquarters. They now have facilities for cooking and eating, and two hot showers.

On the plateau are numerous peasant houses and two manor houses. All of these are only earthworks, but the outline of walls can be traced, as well as 'hollow ways' which were the routes of communication by foot, animal, or cart through the village, and from it to other places. Beyond all these areas of buildings, enclosures and roadways were the open fields cultivated by the villagers.

All this is to be seen on the surface, but underneath this are the remains of earlier settlements going back to prehistoric times, which only excavation has revealed. To gain some understanding of how these were discovered, we have to return now to our 'changing problem orientation' and ask how the original question, 'When was the village deserted?' gave way to other more complex modes of enquiry.

Changing problems

The first ten years' work were devoted to the very careful excavation of a peasant house. The question of date quickly gave way to research on house structure and on the standard of living of the Wharram peasant, which was surprisingly high to judge by the range and quality of his material possessions, as found by archaeology.

It was found that the latest house on the site chosen was of the fifteenth century AD, but that below this, in slightly different places and on different orientations, were earlier peasant houses going back to the thirteenth century. High hopes were entertained of carrying the sequence back to Anglo-Saxon times but, very surprisingly, below the earliest peasant house was the filled-in basement or cellar of a well-built stone manor house of the twelfth century (not that represented by other earthworks). The implications were clear: there had been radical changes in village layout during the medieval period, and it could no longer be maintained that the visible earthwork plan was 'as it always had been'.

This was the first major change in Wharram's research direction. The next was the church. Although another peasant house on the plateau was dug (and this did go back to earlier timber structures) the main effort was now on the church.

Although the settlement as such was abandoned and given over to sheep farming in the fifteenth century, the church continued to be the place of worship and burial for those of the surrounding settlements that had survived. The last recorded burial was in 1909, and the last service was held in 1949. In the 1950s thieves robbed the roof of its lead and it soon became ruinous. In 1959 half of the tower collapsed, and this was the impetus for the archaeologists to take an interest in the church – another major step away from the peasants and their houses. The rubble was recorded and what remained of the church was made safe from further falls.

The church was totally excavated inside and out, together with associated burials, and the whole structure was drawn stone by stone. The plans of several earlier churches were recovered, and it was shown that the earliest phase, and the earliest burials, were of late Saxon date (though not necessarily contemporary).

The church in its various stages of building, rebuilding, expansion, and final contraction was important in its own right as the spiritual nucleus of the settlement for many centuries. But it was also a microcosm of the changing fortunes of both the village and its lords. It also provided the first data, in the form of skeletons, on the villagers and lords themselves, and also their priests. These were able to give information on public health and nutrition, age expectancy, infant mortality and disease. Over 600 graves have now been dug, out of a total of 5–8000 people who are estimated to have been buried at Wharram. Of these, only a maximum of 38 are now marked by memorial stones (Rahtz and Watts, 1983).

Horizons were expanded further when, below the lowest church levels, pottery was found of the Iron Age and Roman periods, showing that Wharram did not originate as a medieval village. Further work in the valley during the 1970s included a large excavation of the medieval fish-pond dam and, below this, the remains of the mill-ponds of Saxon date, though all remains of the actual mills had been destroyed, swept away by flooding or removed by later medieval structures such as the fish-ponds. These excavations widened the scope of enquiry into the technology of milling and fish-farming. Further excavations carried the Wharram story forward in time into the post-medieval centuries with the study of the eighteenth-century vicarage and farm. Details of these, recovered by archaeology, correspond with and corroborate (but vastly enlarge on) the details given in contemporary written sources.

These large-scale excavations had been very informative about particular areas and structures, but there were still large parts of the site about which nothing was known. The change to guardianship status gave greater opportunities to explore more widely, and in the 1970s a series of trial trenches was dug in many parts of the village. The results were startling. Not only did they reveal widespread evidence of Anglo-Saxon, Roman and Iron Age occupation, but showed that the very plan of the earthworks, which had been assumed to be a medieval creation, had its origins in the Roman and pre-historic periods. Roman ditches and banks were found to underlie medieval ones, and a major linear boundary marking the ends of peasant properties was shown to be a prehistoric field bank. It was now clear that Wharram had been intensively occupied for at least a thousand years before the medieval village and its earthworks which had sparked off the original research. The great attraction for settlers was probably the excellent water supply.

The next stage was the realization that, however interesting all this might be for the 'site' of Wharram Percy (whose limits were now by no means so certain as they had been), we needed to see if the site was typical of the area, and to set it into a wider context. This was done in two ways: intensive aerial photography which showed in soil crop-marks the outlines of former fields, settlements and buildings; and systematic walking over all the ploughed fields within 5 kilometres of Wharram Percy. Pottery and other finds of all periods were picked up and their positions mapped. This helped to date the air-photograph markings, and to plot the position and extent of occupation in different places in the Iron Age, Roman, Saxon and medieval periods.

By these two methods of non-excavational field-work among other sites, two Roman villas were discovered, both within 2 kilometres of Wharram Percy itself. Fragments of mosaic, painted plaster, tiles from heating systems, and other finds indicated the high status of these sites. We began to realize that settlement in the area in the Roman period may have been more intensive than at any time before or since.

A further technique was now employed to find out more about the villas. A survey of both sites was done using a magnetometer. This is a device which measures the magnetic response of buried finds and features. It can pick up hearths, ditches, pits, walls, roads and other features by recording their different magnetic response to that of the natural chalk. It was possible in both cases to recover the extent and entire plan of both sites in outline, though not to date the individual components. (Figure 7 indicates the result from one of the villas.)

A further stage was to excavate a series of small holes on both villas. In 1979, in only four days and with a dozen workers, the evidence of field-walking, aerial photography and magnetometer survey was much enhanced. Elements of the buildings were found which showed the range of materials used and the dating range. Ditches were sectioned to find their depth and date; and again prehistoric occupation was proved, extending back, in the case of the villa illustrated, to mesolithic flints of thousands of years before the Roman period.

Current work

We were now able to set our Wharram Percy finds into an outline settlement pattern for the surrounding area. Area excavations continued on the main site. Currently, the two principal ones are on the two manorial sites. By the South Manor (where earlier the stone basement with superimposed peasant houses had been found) an extensive area of the middle Saxon period (eighth–ninth century AD) has been discovered, including a Saxon smithy. More pottery of this period has been found in this area than in the whole of the rest of the north of England put together.

Since I joined the dig, the University of York's own patch has been the other (North) Manor, where we have just completed five seasons with our students. We have been very

WHARRAM LE STREET. N.YORKS.
Magnetometer survey. 1978.

> 25 gamma anomalies
10 - 25 " "
< 10 " "

?location of building   K : ?kiln
grid pegs

N

METRES

0   10   100

FEATURES NAMED BY P.A.R. 1982 IN ITALIC

AML.AB. 1979

Figure 7 Wharram-le-Street North Yorks, Magnetometer Survey, 1978.

fortunate here in recovering a sequence which is almost like a microcosm of the whole Wharram complex.

The earliest features apart from some Neolithic stone finds, are large ditches of the pre-Roman Iron Age (first century BC). These were of several phases, and included an entrance causeway. It seems likely that this is the edge of a large defended pre-Roman farm that lies under the medieval manor. Was there continuity here over a period of thirteen centuries? Only a very large excavation could prove or disprove this.

We also found that a hollow way (a worn-down track or road) which traversed the edge of our area originated in the Iron Age. It was also extensively used in the Roman period. Of Roman date also was a corn-drying oven by the side of the road, and many Roman finds of coins, pottery and metal. There were also some *tesserae* (cubes from mosaic) and some very large stone blocks. These hint that nearby is a third Roman villa to add to the two that had been found by field-walking and aerial photography.

There was then a very sharp break. The Roman road was cut away by two Anglo-Saxon buildings of the sixth–seventh century AD, obviously marking an abrupt change in at least the patterns of communication; more pottery and a few post-holes of later centuries take the use of the site forward to that of the medieval manor of the twelfth century. The road had by now come back into use, and was the principal road from the village to the nearby market town of Malton, where it had also led in Roman times. Malton was an important fort and settlement.

This remarkable sequence, recovered in only 400 square metres of excavation, illustrates very well the potential of Wharram Percy as a multi-period site, and how far we have progressed from the simple questions, 'When was the village deserted, and how did its peasants live?'

Training and theory

Although Wharram, and in particular our own excavation area of the North Manor, is part of my own research at York,

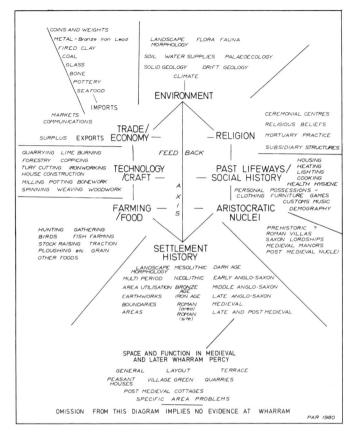

Figure 8 Wharram Data and Interpretation.

we also use it to train our students. Here, in the summer season, they learn how to excavate and draw, fill out recording forms, and process the thousands of finds of all kinds from pottery to animal bones. But because it is part of an academic course, and not just a field school in practical archaeology, we have attempted to express the whole Wharram project in a theoretical framework, shown here as figure 8. Not surprisingly this was received with indifference, if not apathy, by the 'old hands' at Wharram, Academic theory doesn't seem very relevant to anything when you're actually digging; there is always a big gulf between the academic theorizer and the men in the field, doing the job.

For the students, however, concepts such as those expressed in the diagram help them to gain a perspective of the whole project and its importance, even when what they are doing day by day is only a tiny fragment of the whole. Figure 8 represents a *systemic* approach to the massive Wharram data, rather than a *chronological* one. Here we're not dealing successively with Iron Age people, Romans, Saxons and medieval peasants and lords, but with the systems that operate with society, each of them having complex links and interaction with others.

Such systems and their interaction may be seen in modern society. In York, the city runs through the efficient management of many interlinking systems: the legal system with its police and courts; the ecclesiastical systems of its cathedral and churches; the commercial systems of banking and commerce; the academic systems of its university and schools; its social systems of heat, light, sewage, hospitals and welfare; the trading systems dealing with long-distance luxury imports (such as Japanese TV sets) and its mundane food and drink, distributed on a more local basis and involved in a complex symbiosis with the rural hinterland.

Add to these the systems of transport, industry and (in York especially) tourism and archaeology, and we begin to build a theoretical framework to explain how York works. It would be relatively straightforward to depict present-day York systems, and one could from written sources build up a similar framework (changing all the time) back through the nineteenth and eighteenth centuries to Tudor times. As we go further back through time, written sources become more sparse, and for medieval, Viking and Roman York, the archaeologists hope to build a picture of York's earlier systems based almost wholly on archaeological evidence. It would in York be far more complex than that for Wharram, but similar in the type of theoretical framework within which the data are considered.

The present excavations at Wharram, extensive though they are, and extending over 35 years, have explored less than 5 per cent of the site. In the present academic and financial climate of opinion, it is unlikely that there will be any more excavations after 1990, though it will take several more years for all the work to be fully published. By 1990, the present directors will (at best) be at the end of their active working life. Although there might be younger people who would be prepared to take over from the old men, some current feeling is that this generation has had its 'bite' of the Wharram cake. A site as safe as this, free from any threat of ploughing or development, should be preserved for future generations who may be better equipped to excavate and publish. Many people believe that any resources of money and manpower would be better spent on deserted villages that are gradually being destroyed by modern farming.

Meanwhile Wharram will remain as a monument, a unique opportunity for the general public to see and study all aspects of a prehistoric, Roman, Saxon and medieval settlement in its chronological and landscape setting. Most of what will be visible will be of medieval date. The experience of visiting Wharram will be a valuable counterbalance to the partial impression people get of medieval daily life by visiting castles, religious houses and other major buildings which were used by only the few.

9

Archaeology and the Public

Archaeology has a series of different publics at varying levels of appreciation. All of them put together are a very small minority of the population. The dialogue between archaeologists and their publics is complex in motive, media and method. The vast majority of the public are not only not interested in archaeology as a method of understanding the past, they are not interested in the past. A farmer on Sanday (one of the north isles of Orkney, an area where one might expect an interest in tradition and 'old days') confessed to me (or rather aserted) that he was more interested in the future: in 'computers, space, and the supernatural'. This did not stop him from being very helpful to the archaeologists digging on his land.

The relatively small proportion of people who are interested in the past vary in their response to archaeology according to two principal factors – the skill with which archaeologists communicate or expound their subject, and the very diverse levels of public perception about what lies behind present experience. We have already seen the aboriginal concept of only two 'times', the moving present and the ancestral past and it is doubtful whether the majority of people, even in an educated country like Britain, have more than this dual conception of time. 200 years ago, 20,000, 200,000, 2 million, all are much the same in public perception, though critically different for the archaeologist.

162

Radio-carbon 14 is believed to be a pirate radio station. Film audiences are not disturbed by watching Raquel Welch and other early hominids co-inhabiting a landscape with dinosaurs and pterodactyls, in 'One Million Years BC'; or Romans fighting Vikings in 'The Viking Queen'.

At the academic level there are only a few hundred people likely to read or skim most of the papers or monographs I write on archaeology, and those mostly in Britain. An important book with a wide scholarly appeal such as *Models in Archaeology* (Clarke (ed.), 1972), with a wider market in the USA and elsewhere, might sell a few thousand copies. At a more popular level, the book you are reading will be doing well if it reaches a world readership of 10,000, a very small proportion of the world's population, and minute compared to the books of the 'alternative archaeology' (Chapter 7).

Interest in archaeology is not, however, confined to those who read books. The public which archaeology tries to serve and communicate with is potentially the much wider one who listen to radio, watch television, travel and look at 'ancient monuments', visit museums, and look at excavations. The numbers in Britain are possibly a million or two who can be reached in some way. Beyond this there is the great majority, who do none of these things. Most are apathetic to archaeology, or downright hostile when it is seen in their view to be 'wasting public money' or delaying 'progress'. When I was digging the Saxon and medieval palaces at Cheddar, I was held by some of the village community to be delaying the new school (the building of this was the reason for the dig). One of the village councillors said, 'They say they've found King Alfred's palace. Now he was a great believer in education, if he was here he'd say get on with the school' – which was probably true! At the very best, we may cite the recent instance of the estimated British audience of 2.5 million who watched the breakfast-time saga of the lifting of the Tudor warship *Mary Rose* from the seabed.

Half a million, then, is probably our maximum potential public at the most popular level; so far we as archaeologists have been singularly unsuccessful in getting over to them the real interest of archaeology which I hope I have sketched in this book. The reasons for this are discussed later in this chapter. There are many different levels at which we may hope to make any impact. These levels depend on how our public *perceives* archaeology. Generally it is low-key: archaeology is 'about digging up old things, especially treasure'; in many people's minds it's something that happens in other countries, especially in Greece or Egypt. Above all it is *mysterious* at a higher key, *local* archaeology has a considerable appeal, and so do *finds* of all kinds, especially human skeletons.

The public are often puzzled by things they see on digs or hear in lectures. One of the most common questions from visitors is, 'How did all this get buried?' The simple answer here is earthworms, who cast up dirt on any exposed surface at an astonishing rate – one can observe how quickly a path gets buried if not regularly cleared. There is also some material derived from leaves, weeds and frost, which help the earthworm to bury our past.

Although we seem to dig up a lot of people's past rubbish, most of it does *not* get buried, but dispersed and reused or destroyed. What we find is a minute fraction of what was used in the past. Future generations will be more lucky – we put our rubbish in huge dumps, from which the future archaeologists will have a vast harvest of bottles, tins, bedsteads, washing machines and television sets; they will also have a massive documentary record of what these things mean in our society, if our paper, film, and magnetic tape survive. If they don't, the rubbish dumps will be the only source from which our life can be reconstructed, as is the case now for our own prehistory.

Why should we try to reach the public? Why should we not be content to be a minority group, appealing to a small elite, who will appreciate to the full our methods and our subtle approaches to the past?

We do need an informed public; we cannot afford to be isolated. Archaeology needs the understanding and collaboration of the farmer, the gravel-extractor, and the bushman. An informed and interested public will not destroy its own past (our raw data). Legislation to protect monuments or provide resources for archaeology cannot be effective without public support. Local authorities, planning committees and builders must see archaeology as a resource, as strengthening community identity with its region and its heritage. Modern social mobility threatens our roots; archaeology can help us to renew a sense of context without risking the disasters of parochialism or nationalism.

Archaeology is potentially a source of tourist income. Public interest must extend to MPs. Why do birds, poetry, painting and the theatre rank higher in public awareness and government grants? Why is Japan the biggest archaeological spender per head of the population? Academic archaeology is also under threat – in 1982 four archaeology departments in British universities were recommended to close, and two of them did do so. We need public support in all places and at all levels. Readers of this book who have followed me so far will, I hope, have no doubts about the intrinsic interest of archaeology, and its importance in today's world, but we may recapitulate some of the reasons why we should try to get a bigger public, at the risk of some repetition.

EDUCATION OR ENTERTAINMENT?

The wider the public we wish to involve, the more popular our approach must be. It is difficult, however, to lower our sights without vulgarizing, trivializing, or being downright misleading. At worst, in efforts to entertain, some writers and TV presenters have descended to sensationalism or personalization, pandering to the big demand for features on treasure, mummies, skeletons, or mystery. The real excitement of archaeology is a formidable concept to put over in any medium.

Formal education is one way of preparing the ground. From the primary school onwards, the tangible and practical aspects of archaeology, in the classroom or outside in town or country, provide excellent opportunities for the teacher, broadening and deepening the base of history. Many teachers are as uninformed about archaeology as the majority of the public, and since the public's image of archaeology is as a harmless hobby, with odd people digging up things, neither education ministers, committees, headmasters, or teachers are likely to treat archaeology as an important and eminently suitable subject for the curriculum. In secondary education, the position in Britain is rather better. It is possible to take O- and A-level archaeology, and the standards are high; but there are not enough teachers able to take the subject on, or headmasters eager to introduce the subject and find someone to teach it. It was hoped at one time that archaeology might fill the gap in humanist studies left by the decline in classical studies, or that it might take a slice of the history cake; but neither of these things has happened, though valiant attempts are being made. In history, even medieval topics are rarely taught after the first year; Tudors and Stuarts and the nineteenth century still reign supreme, a very small and recent part of Britain's past.

We are left with tertiary education, with 20–30 universities in Britain offering various degrees, of archaeology by itself or in conjunction with other appropriate subjects, notably history, and to a lesser extent, geology or geography. Some universities, notably Bradford, have an important scientific bias, and offer BSc rather than BA degrees. For the very best students, there are ample opportunities for postgraduate research. Few students know very much about archaeology when they come from school; perhaps 5 per cent have taken archaeology O- or A-levels. Thirty per cent or more have, however, 'been on a dig', and this is usually crucial in having persuaded them to read archaeology.

The range of courses available is very wide, ranging from scientific archaeology to historically-based studies, from the earliest hominids and stone tools to post-medieval archaeology and ethnoarchaeology, and from British-based courses to ones that cover the archaeology of more distant areas, especially North West Europe and the Mediterranean, but including Egypt, the Far East, Polynesia, Australia and the Americas. Readers of this book who are thinking of studying archaeology should make themselves well informed about what is on offer.

An informed public is essential if archaeology is to survive as a subject, and equally importantly if its subject-matter, its sites above and below ground, are to survive the destructive agencies of nature and modern industrial society. Debates about the provision of resources for archaeology at local authority or central government level are frighteningly ill-informed.

It is not surprising, therefore, that public knowledge of archaeology is so slight, compared with that in some other countries, notably Scandinavia, Holland and Switzerland. The subject can only be promoted in the future by the few hundred graduates turned out by British universities each year. They can and do do a great deal to make people around them better informed, by talking and teaching. Those that get into jobs in archaeology can do a great deal more, in campaigning for more resources, awakening local authorities to the value of their archaeological heritage, persuading farmers and metal-detectors not to destroy the past wantonly for the sake of profit, and monitoring or hopefully recording the ravages of nature.

SANDAY

An excellent example of what can be done at the local level is provided by Sanday, an island in the northern part of Orkney, which I observed while I was writing this chapter. Sanday has a population of just over 500. Like most of Orkney it is extremely rich in archaeological sites, ranging from Neolithic chambered tombs through Bronze Age, Pictish and Norse settlement sites to its medieval and modern farms. Many of the latter are on or near the sites of their predecessors. Unlike some of the better-known Orkney islands, which are extensively visited by tourists, and with famous sites (such as the Neolithic village of Skara Brae, the Neolithic tomb of Maes Howe, and stone circles), Sanday

167

was hardly known to tourists, and its archaeology was until recently neglected. It was left to the Orkney field archaeologist, Raymond Lamb, to survey the island, talk to its farmers and make them aware of their island history. What makes Sanday unique, and which gives the island its name, are the extensive dunes and areas of blown sand which have buried well-preserved ancient sites. In places this has happened several times, so that there are up to 2–3 metres of archaeological deposits extending through four thousand years. There are also many large mounds of soil and midden deposits, rather like the tells of the Middle East, which have either been built up deliberately, or have accumulated through time. On and in these are the well-preserved stone structures of Norse and later farms. All this rich archaeology is being steadily destroyed, not by the farmers of Sanday, but by the sea. Huge storms sweeping in from the Atlantic whip up great waves, which not only sometimes flood the coastal farms, but tear into the low cliffs and into their deep archaeological deposits. In one winter, up to ten metres of land has been lost in places, representing thousands of tons of archaeological levels. To Lamb this was a situation that demanded action. With the goodwill secured by his public relations exercise with the Sanday people, he arranged for a large-scale dig to be done by John Hunter, of the University of Bradford. In 1983 Hunter opened quite large areas behind the sea-eroded cliff, and demonstrated the great potential of the site in Pictish and Norse times, with well-preserved stone buildings and a wealth of artefacts. The islanders were impressed and convinced about their island's past. When the dig was finished, Hunter produced an illustrated report in the form of a four-page newspaper. A copy of this was delivered to every home on the island. In April 1984, a conference of Scottish archaeologists was held on Sanday for five days (the reason for my own visit). The warmth of the islanders' hospitality and the extent of their interest in archaeology was a remarkable experience. Many of the islanders came round with us on our excursions, and 30–40 of them came to the lectures in their village hall on all aspects of their past, from the Neolithic tombs and settlements to the Jacobite rebellion in Orkney, and modern farming practice. Of especial interest to them was the archaeological evidence for the production of kelp, which brought great wealth to Orkney, and Sanday in particular, in the later eighteenth and early nineteenth centuries. Seaweed is burnt to produce an ashy residue used in glass-making, and later in the manufacture of iodine.

Sanday is an example of what can be done at a *local* level, but is of little help in reaching our wider potential audience or public.

MEDIA, MUSEUMS AND MONUMENTS

Formal education and public relations exercises like Sanday can lay foundations for a public interest in archaeology, but they have limited scope. The more indirect role of public presentation is potentially vastly greater, especially through the media, which can reach virtually the whole world population in one way or another. But the media are under the control neither of archaeologists nor even academics, who may in any case be quite unqualified to put archaeology across.

In Britain, newspapers report archaeology in a very small way, principally at the local level – the local find or dig, emphasizing the sensational or the personal. Even when an archaeologist gives the reporter a careful tour of the dig, or gives him a written account, the result after editing is seldom satisfactory, or even accurate. Even the *Guardian* and the *Telegraph*, in reporting the remarkable find recently in York of an eighth century Anglo-Saxon helmet, managed to turn it into a *Viking* helmet in their columns. Sunday colour supplements have been of great value in carrying illustrated reports of big excavations such as York or London and crises in the funding of British archaeology, or in the destruction of the archaeological heritage. We have some good allies here. *The Illustrated London News* has a long-standing involvement with archaeology.

Radio has put out several series on archaeology. The producer of the BBC *Origins* programme claims to have a big audience. In a recent lecture in York, he played extracts from programmes to persuade the audience that the spoken word can convey visual images to the listener as successfully as can television or film.

There has yet to be a full-scale commercial film which deals successfully with archaeology. Archaeologists figure as very odd characters in films like *Raiders of the Lost Ark*, which *did* reach a world audience, and *does* depict archaeology being done, even if with the worst of motives and with appallingly crude methods. Most 'archaeological' films are highly imaginative reconstructions of the past (or the future), especially of Vikings, Egyptians, or Romans, often with scant regard for time-sense.

Television is potentially the archaeologist's most effective shop-window. Series such as Kenneth Clark's *Civilisation*, Bronowski's *The Ascent of Man*, and Leakey's *The Making of Mankind* have reached world audiences of many millions. David Attenborough in his *Life on Earth* and *The Living Planet* has been enormously succesful in depicting the history of man's environment and animal life, but he has yet to turn his hand to the history of men; if he did so, we could be assured of a vast public eager to know more. The BBC's *Chronicle* series were notable in former years, but have recently become less effective, with certain notable exceptions, such as Barry Cunliffe's programme on Bath. None of the current series, however, gets anywhere near the enormous success of *Animal, Vegetable and Mineral* in which Mortimer Wheeler became a household name, which people still remember many years later. Wheeler did more than any other single person to popularize archaeology, without ever descending to sensationalism or historical inaccuracy.

The BBC did make one serious attempt to explain the approaches and methods of archaeology in their sustained reporting of the excavation at Silbury Hill, the great cere-monial mound in Wiltshire. This was regarded by BBC producers as a successful educational venture, although 'nothing was found' in any way that might be thought to appeal to a wide public. Peter Fowler may have been underestimating the public when he suggested recently that the only way to have put Silbury over would have been for the BBC to 'plant' in the middle of the mound a 'royal mummy, swathed in gold lamé, and containing a pregnant child-bride richly attired, murdered and headless'.

Other attempts have been less successful. Another well known archaeologist seen in a series of *Chronicle* programmes appeared to be wearing the same Oxfam raincoat in a variety of locations from the Peloponese of Greece to Polynesia. The real idiot prize must, however, go to whoever in Britain's Channel 4 dreamed up the idea of low budget half-hour straight lectures on a recent Sunday midday slot, on archaeological and historical topics. The full-frontal image of the lecturer's face or form was relieved only occasionally by a shot of a map or a picture postcard, or a shot of an audience which appeared to consist of four or five bored young people pulled in off the street or rented from an agency.

Museums have traditionally been the institutions where the public went if they wanted to know about the past. For over a century they have fulfilled this role with varying success. Most are still object-orientated, giving the impression that the past is represented by finds rather than about the understanding of settlement or the environment. The finds were and are often in glass cases, untouchable and remote, with little explanation. Especial emphasis is given to rich finds of gold and silver, and other exotic materials. To the academic archaeologist, these displays are of great interest, and we visit museums all over the world to see this material culture. The more old-fashioned, crowded and unselective the display the more we like it (within limits), the more there is to study, photograph, and note. But for the public, this is a quite ineffective mode of stimulation or enlightenment. If you doubt this, sit in a gallery in one of the more archaic museums and watch the public drift by as though they were only sheltering from the rain (they probably are). Lord Montagu, Chairman of the English Tourist Board, and now of the new HBMC was well aware of this when he recently attacked Britain's top museums. He dismissed their curators as 'crusty and pompous'; 'the more honours they have, the duller they are.'

Things are, however, looking up. More and more museums have lots of pictures, explanations, brilliant display and lighting, audio/visual displays, models of excavations, and reconstructions in pictures or three dimensions of early buildings or settlements. Notable here are the great ship museums, the National Maritime Museum at Greenwich, the Oslo Ship Museum, that at Roskilde in Denmark, and the museum built around the seventeenth-century warship *Wasa* at Stockholm. The public also feel especially drawn to museums of more recent times, with which they can identify, such as the ever-popular Castle Museum in York which includes a complete nineteenth-century street with its shops, and a vast collection of 'bygones'. Also in York is the great National Railway Museum, with huge shining locomotives and evocative displays of the Age of Steam.

However good these displays are, they are however static, with at best a few science museum working models, or coin-in-the-slot 'scenes' such as the grisly public execution in York Castle Museum. The new museum concept is very different, and will be vastly more effective in public education, as I have mentioned in relation to Sturbridge Old Village and the Jorvik Viking Centre. This was created by a new breed of museum men, 'leisure engineers' or, as they call themselves, 'imagineers'. At its opening in April 1984, we were given some of the first rides in the time-cars, and then treated to a magnificent feast provided, and flown in by Iceland Air, superb Icelandic fish, roast lamb, curd and blueberries. Our host was another successful 'front man', Magnus Magnusson, himself an Icelander. The Jorvik Viking Centre is only the beginning. Similar projects are being planned for an underground mining museum, and a Roman port.

Our monuments are also archaic in their appeal to the public. To quote Peter Addyman, the Director of the York Archaeological Trust:

Almost all of the 399 national monuments are crying out for this kind of treatment, but the imagination has not been there. Now we have the technology – we can bring more people to Stonehenge without destroying it.

We have convinced ourselves that we have a duty to put the heritage across in an interesting and exciting way. It belongs to all of us, and it is too important to be left to the scholars, the museums, and the experts with unreadable guide books. When I go to Stonehenge now I'm appalled by the squalor of it – the dirty, crowded car parks, the ropes, the muddy paths, the aimless crowds. With £6 million, we could take in more visitors, tell them more, make Stonehenge look better, preserve the vitally important surrounding landscape, and still provide jobs and make a profit.

This is what the new Historic Buildings and Monuments Commission is all about, to make our heritage understood by all, and to make it *pay* – even though the aims are rather contrasting in their ethics.

However successful we are or may be in promoting understanding of archaeology or of the past, we are not reaching or going to reach the great majority, those who *don't* go to the Jorvik Viking Centre, who *pass* the doors of museums, who *switch off* the radio or TV when there is anything even remotely cultural. We write for the *Observer*, the *Guardian*, the *Telegraph*, The *Times*; but not for the *Sun, Star,* or *Mirror*. Here we may justly be accused of being elitist. This may be one reason for the hostility shown to archaeology not only by the irrationalists, but by the metal-detectors.

Tony Gregory is a Norfolk archaeologist who is one of the few archaeologists to have been understanding and sympathetic to the metal-detector users. He has even enrolled them in field-work, searching the ploughsoil over wide areas to plot and recover metal objects which can give clues about buried sites; he lectures to their meetings, and explains the importance of knowing exactly where finds come from and what can be learnt from them by careful study and especially by finding them in context. He believes that the success of metal-detecting is that it is opposed to the middle-class and elitist world of archaeology. It is a *working-class* movement: the finding of ancient objects, and the finding-out about them, may be the only insight into the past that the metal-detectors get. Very often this will lead them into a real interest in archaeology. This generalization does not of course apply to the small minority, the 'night-hawks' who pillage sites in the darkness for financial gain.

It may well be that archaeology is on the verge of a big boom, as there is increasing leisure/unemployment, and a search for roots and a 'natural' past in an increasingly contaminated and industrialized world. The problems of saturation visiting of monuments, their wearing away by millions of feet, however distasteful this may be to the high-minded archaeologist, are probably less worrying than the gradual disappearance of any interest in the past or its heritage, and the exclusive concentration on today's and tomorrow's material world.

ARCHAEOLOGY AND YOU

As a reader of this book, you are one of a small minority. You will have had *some* interest in archaeology, enough to pick up this book idly, or even (hopefully) to buy it. So I have been preaching to at least the semi-converted (unless you read it to find out how to destroy archaeology). I hope, however, that whatever the level of your interest in archaeology when you read my Preface, you are now *more* interested and aware of the subject's absorbing interest and human relevance. You may even feel like reading more, or getting personally involved. If this is the case, how do you set about it?

The first thing is to watch television, listen to radio and above all read as much as possible. Subscribe to popular periodicals to give you the flavour of the archaeological world and what goes on in it.

Visit your local museum, go to any meetings, conferences, excursions, or lectures they may arrange. Get to know the staff; find out what's going on in your area; what local societies there are that you could join, what field-work or excavation is being done that could use your help. Similar information can often be found in your local library or archaeological unit or even university department – we get many enquiries from people like you!

Make your talents known: can you take good photographs, have you a knowledge of surveying or geology, are you tough enough to go out in all weathers, can you type, can you draw, can you stand boring clerical jobs, can you use a computer, can you bake a good cake or jam tarts, or brew beer or wine? If you can do any of these, you will be welcomed with open arms, especially if you don't want any money. It's your *time* and *skills* that are needed. Don't take 'no' for an answer: archaeologists are not always kindly, courteous, tolerant, or even polite – they can be astonishingly rude and offputting. Develop a thick skin and be persistent, and before you know where you are, you will *be* an archaeologist, and inviting others to join you, in the same way as I have invited you.

What I have just outlined is the role of the amateur in archaeology, or rather the amateur beginning; amateurs can become very 'professional'.

You may, however, wish to go further and be a profesional archaeologist, in the sense of getting paid to do archaeology. It used to be possible to get into archaeology without any training or qualifications (as I did). In Britain this has become increasingly difficult but there may well be openings in other countries where there is a shortage of archaeologists. To get any further in Britain, you have to have a lot of experience, publications and reputation, which is difficult to acquire, or you must embark on training. We have seen in Chapter 4 how to do this, and in Chapter 5 what it is like to be a student. Not all students are fresh from school. Some are 'mature' students, of all ages from 21 to 50+. Graduation takes three years, and there are postgraduate courses, such as museum studies at Leicester. If you are talented and motivated enough you may work your way into an archaeological career, as a digger or field-worker, a museum curator, a local authority archaeologist, or an academic. You could end up by being as famous as Barry Cunliffe, or Mortimer Wheeler. What did they have at your age that you haven't got? What they *didn't* have was the stimulation of having read this book!

175

Conclusion

Many readers of this book, even if they have found it stimulating and enjoyable, will not have found in it the answers to all the questions in their minds when they bought it. Many important aspects of archeology are hardly mentioned, notably the practical aspects – tools, techniques, stratigraphy, survey, and other things inseparable from modern archaeology. There is little on finds, or on the many scientific and specialist skills which are increasingly being brought to bear on our evidence. There are many new kinds of archaeology which the reader of this book may remain unaware of, such as industrial and marine (underwater) archaeology. I can only repeat that this is not meant to be a textbook, but a personal view of the relevance of archaeology to the world of today. Readers who want to find out how to 'do' archaeology are referred to other books listed below.

The only missing chapter which I would like to have written is 'archaeology in the future', if indeed it has one. I have written about today's rubbish, but not how future archaeologists will deal with it. Speculation here really belongs to the world of science fiction, and certain developments are hinted at in Chapter 7. I shall not be here to see the exciting developments that the twenty-first century will bring to our discipline, on this earth or beyond. But I hope that there are enough young readers to see these new things happen, and to be able to look back at this book and say 'this is what it was like in the 1980s'.

Further Books to Read

Leslie Alcock *Arthur's Britain* (Pelican, Harmondsworth, 1974): this will help you to understand the Dark Age sections in this book.

David Baker *Living with the Past* (David Baker, Bedford, 1984): a lively book on the problems of caring for the historic environment in modern planning.

Philip Barker *Techniques of Archaeological Excavation* (Batsford, London, 1977): a classic book on the complexity and subtlety of modern excavation.

Rupert Bruce-Mitford *The Sutton Hoo Ship Burial: A Handbook* (2nd edn) (British Museum, London, 1972): an introduction to the richest single archaeological group ever found in Britain; the material from the 1939 excavation (see Chapter 8).

John Coles *Experimental Archaeology*: few archaeologists try, as Coles does, to find out how things worked in the past; modern replicas are made of weapons, buildings are erected and burnt down, to gain more understanding of the evidence that archaeologists find.

James Deetz *Invitation to Archaeology* (Natural History Press, New York, 1967): this book's namesake, and still a very good introduction to modern theoretical archaeology.

Peter Fowler *Approaches to Archaeology* (Black, 1977): a lively and entertaining book and one of the first to explore some of the topics developed in this volume.

Kevin Greene *Archaeology: An Introduction* (Batsford, London, 1983): the most recent of textbooks on archaeology and very readable; it even includes a picture of Raquel Welch.

Barri Jones *Past Imperfect* – the Story of Rescue Archaeology (Heinemann, London, 1984): a recent account of the problems faced by archaeologists in the 1960s and 1970s as they saw their evidence being destroyed faster than it could be recorded.

Richard Leakey *The Making of Mankind* (Michael Joseph, London, 1981): the book of the BBC series; how and why man began, and whether he will prove to be a short-lived species.

Bryony Orme *Anthropology for Archaeologists* (Duckworth, London, 1981): an introduction to the relationship between these two subjects.

Philip Rahtz (ed.) *Rescue Archaeology* (Pelican Books, Harmondsworth, 1974): how our archaeological heritage was being destroyed ten years ago; it is still being eroded by the same agencies of man and nature.

Colin Renfrew *Before Civilisation* (Pelican Books, Harmondsworth, 1973): the *big* perspective, showing the dramatic impact of modern radio–carbon dating.

Andrew Sherratt (ed.) *The Cambridge Encyclopaedia of Archaeology* (Cambridge University Press, Cambridge, 1980): an even *bigger* perspective of man in space and time, covering the world for five million years.

Mortimer Wheeler *Archaeology from the Earth* (Clarendon Press, Oxford, 1954): although 30 years old, this book shows Wheeler's tremendous flair and capacity to communicate.

Current Archaeology: obtainable by subscription (six issues a year) from 9 Nassington Road, London NW3 2TX.

Popular Archaeology: a monthly journal widely distributed through newsagents.

Newsletter and Calendar of the Council for British Archaeology (112 Kennington Road, London, SE11 6RE): this provides a commentary on what is going on in British archaeology, and details of awards, prizes, and – most usefully – details of excavations or summer schools which you can join, even as a beginner, and possibly get part of the costs of food or travel reimbursed.

Bibliography

Adams, D. *The Hitch-Hiker's Guide to the Galaxy* (Pan Books, London, 1979)

Alcock, L. *Arthur's Britain* (Pelican, Harmondsworth, London, 1974)

Ashe, G. *The Glastonbury Tor Maze* (Glastonbury, 1979)

Asimov, I. *The Foundation Trilogy* (New York, 1964)

Bailey, R. 'Dowsing for Medieval Churches', *Popular Archaeology* (February 1983) 33–37

Barker P.A. *Techniques of Archaeological Excavation* (Batsford, London, 1977).

Bonnichsen, R. 'Millie's Camp: An Experiment in Archaeology', *World Archaeology* **4**.3 (February 1973) 277–91

Boulle, P. *Monkey Planet* (USA)

Briggs, H.D., Cambridge, E. and Bailey, R. 'A New Approach to Church Archaeology: Dowsing, Excavation and Documentary Work at Woodhorn, Ponteland and the pre-Norman Cathedral at Durham', *Archaeol. Aeliana*, Fifth ser, **11** (1983) 79–100

Bruce-Mitford, R.L.S. *The Sutton Hoo Ship Burial: A Handbook* (2nd edn) (British Museum, London, 1972)

Burrow, I. and Rahtz, P. in M. Aston and I. Burrow (eds) *The Archaeology of Somerset* (Somerset County Council, Taunton, 1982)

Butzer, K. *Archaeology as Human Ecology* (Cambridge University Press, Cambridge, 1982)

Carver, M. *Bulletin of the Sutton Hoo Research Committee No. 1* (University of Birmingham, Birmingham, April 1983)

Clark, G. *Archaeology and Society* (Methuen, London, 1965)

Clarke, D.L. (ed.) *Models in Archaeology* (Methuen, London, 1972).

Daniel, G.E. *150 Years of Archaeology* (Duckworth, 1975)

Davies, N. *Voyagers to the New World, Fact or Fantasy* (1979)

Deetz, J. *Invitation to Archaeology* (Natural History Press, New York, 1967)

Fagan, B. 'Chairman Mao's Archaeology' in *Quest for the Past* (Addison-Wesley, London, 1978)

179

Fahtz, R. 'The Martian Expedition to Wharram Percy', in D. Hooke (ed.) *New Approaches to Medieval Rural Settlement* (Oxford, 1985)

Fowler, P. *Approaches to Archaeology* (Black, 1977)

Golding, W. *The Inheritors* (Faber & Faber, London, 1955)

Golding, W. *The Spire* (Faber & Faber, London, 1964)

Greene, K. *Archaeology: An Introduction* (Batsford, London, 1983)

Hawkes, J. *Mortimer Wheeler, Adventurer in Archaeology* (Weidenfeld & Nicolson, London, 1982)

Hodder, I. *The Present Past* (Batsford, London, 1982)

Horsman, R. 'Origins of Racial Anglo-Saxonism in Great Britain before 1850', *J. Hist. Ideas* **37** (1976) 387–410

Journal of Galactic Archaeology (first issue awaiting data)

Kennedy, G. *Invitation to Statistics* (Martin Robertson, Oxford, 1983)

Kilworth, G. 'Let's Go to Golgotha' in *The Gollancz/Sunday Times Best SF Stories* (1975)

Leakey, R.E. *The Making of Mankind* (Michael Joseph, London, 1981)

Lodge, D. *The British Museum is Falling Down* (Penguin, Harmondsworth, 1965)

Macaulay, D. *The Mystery of the Motel* (Hutchinson, London, 1979)

Maltwood, K.A. *A Guide to Glastonbury's Temple of the Stars* (Privately published, London, 1935)

Maltwood, K.A. *Air View Supplement to Maltwood 1935* (Privately published, London, 1937)

Mongait, A.L. *Archaeology in the USSR* (Pelican Books, Harmondsworth, 1961)

Orme, B. *Anthropology for Archaeologists* (Duckworth, London, 1981)

Radford, C.A.R. and Swanton, M.J. 'Tintagel' in *Arthurian Sites in the West* (University of Exeter, Exeter, 1975)

Rahtz, P. 'Excavations at Chalice Well, Glastonbury', *Proc. Somerset Archaeol. Nat. Hist. Soc.* **108** (1964) 145–63

Rahtz, P.A. 'Excavations on Glastonbury Tor 1964-66', *Archaeol.J.* **127** (1971) 1–81

Rahtz, P.A. (ed.) *Rescue Archaeology* (Pelican Books, Harmondsworth, 1974)

Rahtz, P.A. *The Saxon and Medieval Palaces at Cheddar* Brit. Archaeol. Rep. 65 (Oxford, 1979)

Rahtz, P.A. (ed.) 'Sutton Hoo Opinions – Forty Years On' in P. Rahtz, T. Dickinson and L. Watts (eds) *Anglo-Saxon Cemeteries 1979,* Brit. Archaeol. Rep. 82 (Oxford, 1979) 313–270

Rahtz, P.A. 'Medieval Milling', in D.W. Crossley (ed.) *Medieval Industry,* Counc. Brit. Archaeol. Res. Rep. 40 (1981) 1–15

Rahtz, P.A. 'Celtic Society in Somerset, AD 400–700', *Bulletin of the Board of Celtic Studies* **30** (1982) 176–200

Rahtz, P. and Bullough, D. 'The Parts of an Anglo-Saxon Mill', *Anglo-Saxon England* **6** (1977) 15–37

Bibliography

Rahtz, P. and Hirst, S. *Beckery Chapel, Glastonbury, 1967–8* (Glastonbury Antiquarian Society Glastonbury, 1974)

Rahtz, P.A. and Watts, L. 'The End of Roman Temples in the West of Britain', in P.J. Casey (ed.) *The End of Roman Britain* Brit. Archaeol. Rep. 71 (Oxford, 1979) 183–210

Rahtz, P. and Watts, L. *Wharram Percy, The Memorial Stones of the Churchyard* (University of York Archaeological Publications, 1, 1983)

Rahtz, P. and Watts, L. 'The Archaeologist on the Road to Lourdes and Santiago de Compostela', in a forthcoming *Festschrift: The Anglo-Saxon Church: papers on architecture, archaeology and history in honour of Dr H.M. Taylor* (eds L.A.S. Butler and R. Morris), Counc. Brit. Archael. Res. Rep. 1985)

Rathje, W.L. 'Le Projet du Garbàge 1975: Historical Trade-offs', in C.L. Redman *et al, Social Archaeology Beyond Subsistence and Dating* (Academic Press, London, 1978)

Renfrew, C. *Before Civilisation* (Pelican Books, Harmondsworth, 1973)

Shackley, M. *Environmental Archaeology* (George Allen & Unwin, London, 1981)

Sherratt, A.L. (ed.) *The Cambridge Encyclopaedia of Archaeology* (Cambridge University Press, Cambridge, 1980)

Silverberg, R. *Up the Line* (New York, 1969)

Twain, M. *A Connecticut Yankee at the Court of King Arthur* (Penguin, Harmondsworth, 1971; first published 1889)

Ucko, P. 'The Politics of the Indigenous Minority', *J. Biosoc. Sci. Suppl.* **8** (1983a) 25–40

Ucko, P. 'Australian Academic Archaeology – Aboriginal Transformations of its Aims and Practices; *Australian Archaeology* **16** (June 1983b) 11–26

Von Däniken, E. *Chariots of the Gods?* (London, 1969)

Vita-Finzi, C. *The Mediterranean Valleys* (Cambridge University Press, Cambridge, 1969)

Westall, R. *The Wind Eye* (Puffin, Harmondsworth, 1976)

Wheeler R.E.M. *Archaeology from the Earth* (Clarendon Press, Oxford, 1954)

White, D. 'Changing Views of the *Adventus Saxonum* in 19th and 20th Century English Scholarship', *J. Hist. Ideas* **37** (1971)

Williamson, T. and Bellamy, L. *Ley Lines in Question* (Tadworth, 1983)

Wilson, A. *Anglo-Saxon Attitudes* (Secker & Warburg, London, 1956)

Index

Index